C000217492

£6-50

SIMON MARKS

RETAIL REVOLUTIONARY

SIMON MARKS

RETAIL REVOLUTIONARY

PAUL BOOKBINDER

WEIDENFELD AND NICOLSON, LONDON

Copyright © Marks and Spencer p.l.c.

First published in Great Britain in 1993 by
George Weidenfeld and Nicolson Ltd
Orion House, 5 Upper St Martin's Lane,
London WC2H 9EA

All rights reserved. No part of this publication
may be reproduced, stored in a retrieval system
or transmitted in any form or by any means,
electronic, mechanical, photocopying or
otherwise, without the prior permission in
writing of the copyright owners.

British Library Cataloguing-in-Publication Data
A catalogue record for this book is available from
the British Library.

ISBN 0 297 83169 0

HOUSE EDITOR: Alice Millington-Drake
DESIGN: Harry Green

Filmset by Selwood Systems, Midsomer Norton
Printed in Great Britain by
Butler & Tanner Ltd, Frome and London

Contents

A Tribute to Paul Bookbinder

Paul Bookbinder died in April 1992 before completing this book. He was approaching his fifty-fifth birthday and was looking forward to marking forty years with the company in 1993.

Having joined us straight from school, Paul served in a variety of management positions in both stores and Head Office. In 1984 he was appointed Company Archivist, in preparation for the company's centenary, assisting Asa (Lord) Briggs with the centenary history, for which he had amassed an extensive archive recording the history of Marks & Spencer and its founders. In 1989, to mark the fiftieth anniversary of the commencement of the Second World War, he produced *Marks & Spencer – The War Years,* a history of the company from 1939 to 1945. He was working on this, his second book, when he died. My colleague Philip Symes and I have attempted to pick up the pieces and have done our best to produce a final version of which Paul would have been proud. The bulk of the work was done by him and I hope it has not been in any way diminished by our contribution.

I know he would have wished us to acknowledge the input of Maureen Murphy, his secretary, for her work in preparing drafts. Philip and I would particularly like to thank Di Lines, who has taken over responsibility for the archive, for her help with additional research. We wish also to express our gratitude to the numerous people within the company, the founding family and outside the business who spent time sharing their memories with us, and undertook their own research on our behalf.

Paul had one personal memory of Simon Marks which he would not have put in the book. One day, while on leave from his national service, he was visiting Marble Arch and saw Simon leave the store. Anxious to make his mark with the great man, he followed him and finally caught up with him on a traffic island in the middle of Oxford Street, where they stood together waiting for the traffic to pass. Overcome by the occasion, Paul finally managed to stammer out nothing more than 'Excuse me, can you tell me the time?', to which Simon replied, 'Young man, there is a clock on the wall up there,' and walked on!

Paul went on to become, owing to his ready wit and larger-than-life personality, a great character of the business, who will long be remembered by those who knew him.

BARRY HYMAN

MARKS FAMILY TREE

Showing only names mentioned in the text

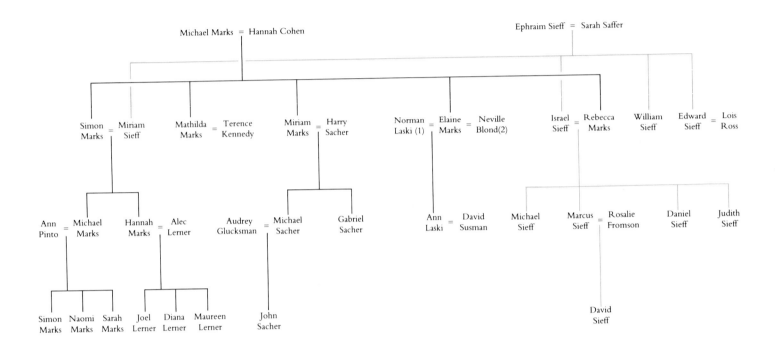

Foreword
By Sir Richard Greenbury

A s a young man in the business learning my trade at Marble Arch, the company's flagship store I, along with countless others, fell under the spell of Simon Marks, unquestionably the retailing genius of this century.

His vision, determination and efforts, ably supported by his lifetime partner, Israel Sieff, created a unique retailing formula which provided the general public for the first time with ranges of high quality, good value merchandise at affordable prices.

Simon Marks's ceaseless striving for business efficiency marched hand-in-hand with both his commercial integrity and his commitment to honest trading and good relation-ships with staff, suppliers and customers.

All who have led the company in the twenty-eight years since his death have remained faithful to the principles with which he imbued every facet of the business. Indeed they are the cornerstones of our success and are as relevant today as ever in the history of the company.

This fascinating book includes the personal accounts of many of the people who knew him, together with a selection of photographs, many published for the first time. It is intended to be a permanent record of a unique individual who is still with us in all we do and achieve.

Sir Richard Greenbury
Chairman
Marks and Spencer p.l.c.

CHAPTER ONE

Beyond the Pale of Settlement

O n Tuesday 7 August 1888, the petite figure of Hannah Marks entered the local registry office in Leeds to register the birth on 9 July of her son Simon. Unable at that time either to read or write a word of English, she made her mark on the birth certificate by inscribing a tiny cross against which the registrar, Mr Bloomfield, added the words 'The mark of Hannah Marks, mother'. He then neatly penned in the baby's birth date, the place of birth – 50 Trafalgar Street, Leeds – and finally the father's occupation as 'Licensed Hawker'. Neither Hannah Marks nor Mr Bloomfield realized that with their completion of the certificate, they had recorded the birth of a future peer of the realm – Simon, Lord Marks of Broughton. While his wife was registering Simon's birth, the baby's father, Michael Marks, was tending his stall in the local market, creating the basis of a business which would later blossom into the retailing empire of Marks & Spencer.

Simon's parents were Jewish immigrants from Russian Poland, who had made their individual ways to England in the early 1880s. They first met in Stockton-on-Tees, on Britain's northeast coast. Michael, visiting the town on business, was forced to take shelter from a downpour in the doorway of a shop near the high street. He soon found himself chatting to a stranger, similarly stranded by the weather, who invited Michael to join him for a meal at his nearby home when the storm had passed. It was there that Michael's host, a Mr Cohen, also an émigré from Russia, introduced Michael to his daughter Hannah. A few months later, on 19 November 1886, the young couple were married under the silken wedding canopy of Leeds's Belgrave Street synagogue. Their wedding certificate gives the bride's age as twenty-one years and the groom's as twenty-two.

The Hebrew marriage certificate (*ketubah*) of Michael Marks and Hannah Cohen; the ceremony took place on 19 November 1886 at the Belgrave Street Synagogue, Leeds.

Michael and Hannah were a well-matched couple, and their marriage was to be a happy and fruitful one. Michael was a hard-working and ambitious man, fiercely determined that his family should never suffer the poverty and privation that he had known during his early life in Russia. Physically, he was lightly built, with a fair, ruddy complexion and a neat, pointed beard; in the words of his future son-in-law Harry Sacher, 'physically not strong, sensitive in spirit, kindly and sympathetic'. Hannah was described by Israel Sieff, another future son-in-law, as 'a wonderful woman . . . a rare creature, small, slight, delicate, devoted. She was, in spite of being small, immensely energetic, a dominating little lady who ruled her husband and her family.'

Michael and Hannah's first child, a boy, died at birth. They were then living in a relatively poor area within the Leeds Jewish community. However, Michael's enterprise at the local Kirkgate Market soon provided them with the necessary funds to move to a more pleasant part of the city. In 1888, just prior to Simon's birth, his parents moved to a small terraced house in Trafalgar Street, a prestigious address in the Leylands district of Leeds, a low-lying area of old houses situated in narrow side streets and alleys not far from the city's main railway station.

Today, a century later, no one lives in Trafalgar Street, and office blocks and industrial

Hannah Marks, Simon's mother. Born Hannah Cohen, the daughter of immigrant parents, she married Michael Marks in 1886 at the age of twenty-one.

Michael Marks, founder of Marks & Spencer and father of Simon. He emigrated from Russian Poland to England in the early 1880s, and began trading in Yorkshire as a pedlar.

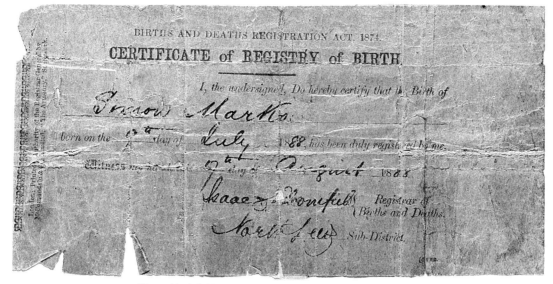

Simon Marks's birth certificate, dated 9 July 1888. At this time neither Michael nor Hannah Marks was able to write in English.

Trafalgar Street, Leeds. Simon was born at No. 50, to the far left of the photograph.

workshops now occupy the sites of houses – including Simon's birthplace. When Hannah and Michael arrived, however, it was the centre of a vibrant, bustling, immigrant community. Jews had lived in Leeds from the eighteenth century, though their numbers did not exceed a few hundred until the 1850s, when tsarist oppression in Russia initiated a steady flow of emigrants to Britain. In 1881, following the assassination of Tsar Alexander II, a particularly bitter persecution of Russia's Jews forced thousands to emigrate. While the majority made their way to the United States, over 100,000 disembarked at Britain's east coast ports between 1881 and 1914.

Some intended only a short stay, before continuing their journey to America, but then for economic reasons or perhaps for fear of the stormy Atlantic, decided to settle in

Britain. A few thousand made for Leeds, where it was rumoured that labour was required for the city's newly emerging mass tailoring industry. This had been reported as far afield as the Jewish heartlands in Russia and Poland. Mass tailoring had developed in Leeds following Isaac Singer's invention of the sewing machine in America. This, coupled with an adaptation of the band saw by Leeds tailor, John Barran, that enabled fabric to be cut in bulk, provided the basis of the new industry.

Soon Jewish tailors and their families were arriving in droves to seek jobs. The city's main railway station was the arrival point for the immigrants, who a few hours earlier had disembarked at the ports of Grimsby or Hull, having travelled for days across northern Europe from their homes in Russia. Wearied and hungry they huddled together on the platforms hoping to meet a welcoming relative or a representative of the local Jewish community.

Local Leeds men, hoping to earn some pocket money as guides, would crowd into the station when the trains arrived, loudly demanding from the immigrants their town of origin – was it 'Lodz? Slonim? Kiev?' Some of the new arrivals carried crumpled scraps of paper bearing the addresses of relatives already living in Leeds, which they would anxiously show the guides. The new arrivals' packs and parcels would then be stacked on the guide's flat handcart, and the group would set off for the stated addresses or for the homes of families known to have originated from the immigrants' home towns. However cramped the accommodation, room would invariably be found for the newcomers, until they were ready to move on.

Although we do not know for certain, Michael Marks may well have arrived in Leeds in such a manner, but there are two accounts of his arrival in Britain. The first, reported in an American-Jewish magazine, describes his landing at Stockton-on-Tees and his taking lodgings with a Jewish family who had emigrated from Russia five years earlier. At his landlord's suggestion, Michael set up as an itinerant pedlar in the villages around Stockton-on-Tees, selling items of smallware from a tray around his neck and a pack on his back. Speaking only Yiddish, and unable at first to understand the British currency, Michael solved his communication problems by having a sign printed on the front of his tray which read 'Don't Ask the Price, it's a Penny'. (He would later use this slogan to great effect when he established his nationwide chain of Penny Bazaars.)

A second, and more likely, account has Michael disembarking at London Docks intending to join his elder brother Barnett who had arrived from Russia some months earlier and was now living in the capital's East End dockland district. To Michael's dismay he discovered that Barnett had, without warning, vacated his lodgings and set sail for the New World to seek his fortune in the gold fields of Canada's Yukon territory. Barnett's hasty departure was apparently occasioned by the attentions of a female admirer, who had pursued him from Russia and was now close to locating him in London. He managed to elude her and set off for the Yukon where he found no gold but later opened a general store in Dawson City. He was eventually to marry, move to Los Angeles, and produce a son, who in later life designed the city's race course. Barnett died in California, well into his nineties.

Michael Marks, meanwhile, now found himself alone in London, where he heard the rumours of the demand in Leeds for unskilled tailors. With just enough money for his train fare, he set off for the north to find work. Whichever account is the true one, within days his arrival in Leeds was noted by a short dapper Yorkshireman named Isaac Dewhirst, who owned a wholesale warehouse close to the city's main market. Mr Dewhirst was standing outside the entrance to his premises with his manager when they were approached by a slightly built, bearded young man who addressed them with the single word 'Barrans'. It was obvious to them that the stranger, Michael Marks, could neither speak nor understand a word of English. Fortunately, Dewhirst's manager Charles Backhouse spoke a little Yiddish, and was able to establish that the penniless young man was hoping to find work at Barrans tailoring factory.

Fate now took a hand, for if Dewhirst had given Michael Marks the directions to the nearby factory, it is most unlikely that Marks would ever have met Isaac Dewhirst's cashier, one Tom Spencer. As it happened, however, in the words of Alistair Dewhirst, Isaac's grandson, 'My Grandfather was fascinated by the stranger. He took him back to his warehouse and offered to lend him five pounds. Michael Marks asked if he might use it to buy goods from the warehouse. My Grandfather agreed and as Michael Marks paid off the debt in instalments, he was allowed to make further purchases to the same amount.' Dewhirst's loan changed Michael's mind about seeking work at Barrans as a tailoring hand. With no assets or skilled training, his choice of a livelihood in Britain was extremely limited, but his chance meeting with Isaac Dewhirst gave him the opportunity to continue the career which had provided his living in Russia – peddling.

Very little equipment was required for such a basic trade, just a canvas backpack for reserve stock and a tray for displaying the penny cotton reels, buttons and ribbons. For two years, Michael the Pedlar, as he became known to his West Riding customers, tramped from house to house or stood on the street corners of villages around Leeds coaxing the pennies from the canny Yorkshire folk. Michael was a born merchant. He enjoyed the twin challenges of seeking out goods that would appeal to his customers and similarly of seeking ways to display his wares to best advantage. He also enjoyed that ultimate thrill of retailing – gauging his success by counting the pennies in his hand at the end of the day's trading.

By 1884, two years before his marriage to Hannah, Michael Marks had graduated from the itinerant life of a pedlar to renting, for one shilling and sixpence, a 6 × 4 ft stall in the open section of Leeds's Kirkgate Market. Apart from providing a more permanent base for his activities – Michael hated travelling far from his home – the stall with its canvas top provided some shelter from the elements, a considerable benefit for one not used to Yorkshire's cold, damp winters. Below the canvas top he hung a sign, painted in yellow letters on a red wooden board, proclaiming 'Marks Penny Bazaar'. Beneath it sat the neatly stocked wickerwork baskets which held the displays of penny items – pins, needles, labels, buttons and haberdashery. Fixed to the uprights were oil lamps, which cast a warm glow over the goods and over the faces of the working-class shoppers who clustered round to buy the latest penny bargains.

By this stage, Marks had learned from his customers that quality and value for money were paramount selling points. While many of his rivals in the market would buy the cheapest goods possible, however shoddy or inferior the merchandise, Marks knew that over the long term this would prove a ruinous policy. He also realized that even if he had been able to speak English, he could not have competed with the promotional banter of neighbouring stallholders. He knew that his goods had to, as it were, speak for him. He therefore had to win the trust of his clientele by selling items that represented value for money. In practical terms this meant buying merchandise from his wholesaler, Isaac Dewhirst, that was of a higher quality – and therefore greater cost price – than the cheapest available. His profits would, he hoped, be maintained by increased turnover.

Isaac Dewhirst, the wholesaler who as a young man lent Michael Marks £5 to purchase stock from his warehouse in Leeds. The firm of I. J. Dewhirst became manufacturers and remain suppliers of Marks & Spencer to this day.

ABOVE Leeds covered market, in front of
the open market, where Michael moved
his business in 1886.

RIGHT A painting of the original Marks'
Penny Bazaar, Michael's first stall in the
open section of the market at Kirkgate,
Leeds, 1884.

By 1888, the year of Simon's birth, this policy was paying off. The crowds around Marks's stall demonstrated his popularity, and other market traders were vying to position their stalls close to his, hoping to benefit from the increased customer flow. Hannah Marks helped her husband during busy periods on the stall. When her apron pockets were bulging with the pennies gathered from the eager customers, she would bag up the cash and carry it to Dewhirst's nearby office for safekeeping. At home, after the evening meal, Hannah would help Michael prepare for the next day's trading by sewing buttons onto display cards and counting the nails, buttons and hairpins into penny bags.

Thus, in the course of a few short years, Michael had not only settled in a new country and learnt its language, he had used his considerable retailing skills to establish the basis of a successful and substantial business. He was regarded by his Leeds kinsfolk as having developed into a 'Mensch', German for 'man', which in Yiddish implied much more, namely an honest and reliable person, a 'real gentleman'.

Caption for engraving:
Engraving, made at a later date, of the interior of the covered market in Leeds.

Simon Marks, Michael's son, unaware of much of his family's early history, wrote towards the end of his life:

> 'I should like to have read a personal account of my great grandfather, how he lived, his work, his thoughts, in fact the story of his life and his family and his memories of his ancestors. There may have been such documents, but the history of our people is one of persecution, sometimes of pogroms and always of retreat, with a burning of synagogues, papers and books. It is not surprising, therefore, that few writings exist.'

Although Simon was born in England and would never visit Russia, he was well aware of the persecution of his Russian ancestors.

In common with millions of other Jews, Simon's forebears originated in the Pale of Settlement, an enormous area of land within the tsarist empire where the tsarist authorities confined their Jewish citizens. It extended from Lithuania in the north to the Black Sea in the south; from the Austro–Hungarian border in the west to the original Russian border some 620 miles to the east. Even within the Pale itself, strategic towns such as Kiev and Yalta were barred to Jews unless they managed to acquire a rare resident's permit. Outside the Pale, Jews, with very few exceptions, were completely barred, the restriction including access to the major cities of Moscow and the capital St Petersburg. Even Jews from outside Russia's borders were not allowed to reside in these cities – in 1886 a distinguished British Jew and parliamentarian Sir Samuel Montagu, later Lord Swaythling, visited Moscow to investigate the situation of Russian Jews, and was obliged by the authorities to leave the city within twenty-four hours.

Anti-Jewish laws proliferated: special taxes, extra-long army service and restrictions on how Jews earned their livelihood were officially enshrined in Russian law. Jews were barred from many of the professions and were in general only allowed to trade as pedlars, tailors or other small-scale craftsmen. Tsarist laws moved Jews from the countryside and into the towns, where many were forced onto the streets as vagrants and beggars. But why this constant harassment and persecution of a basically law-abiding and industrious people, who wished only to live their lives peaceably? The reason was fundamental. In terms of their culture, language, dress, diet and most importantly, their religion, the Jews were stubbornly different from their average Russian or Polish neighbours. To the Russians, the Jews were unwelcome – they had in fact been banned from the country since the end of the fifteenth century.

RIGHT Interior of a synagogue in Slonim, the town in Russian Poland where Michael Marks was born and lived until he emigrated to England.

ABOVE One of a number of synagogues that served the large Jewish community in Slonim. The town lay within the Pale of Settlement, a vast area of land within the Tsarist empire to which Jews were confined. Following the persecution of the Jews after the assassination of Tsar Alexander II in 1881, hundreds of thousands emigrated to the United States of America and England.

RIGHT The Jewish cemetery, Slonim.

It was Russia's gradual expansion into eastern Poland and Lithuania during the late eighteenth and early nineteenth century which brought this area (only later known as the Pale of Settlement), with its one million Jews, under the control of the tsars' double-eagle flag. The Jews had become a nation within a nation and therefore presented a threat to the twin orthodoxies of State and Church.

To the central government, the Jews, along with their business interests to which the State confined them, were considered exploiters of the non-Jewish population and an obstruction to the tsars' ideal of Russification – the concept of one empire, one language and one church. The Orthodox Church, apart from its traditional view of the Jews as the Christ-killers, abhorred the concept of an alien religion usurping their virtual monopoly of the State's official faith. Unprotected by State or Church, the Jews became targets for the mob and the authorities. Over the years hundreds were killed or maimed, their children abducted and brought up as Christians, and their homes put to the torch; 'making the red cock crow' was the Russian peasants' colourful euphemism for such burnings.

Despite the 'pogroms'– Russian for 'devastations' – and the persecutions, the Jews stubbornly survived and even flourished. By the end of the nineteenth century they numbered nearly five million. Within their self-protective solidarity grew a culture, based on religion, which, together with a unique, bitter-sweet style of humour, provided a barrier against the harsh reality of their daily life and the hostility of their neighbours. In their synagogues and homes, the Jews studied and prayed in biblical Hebrew to the one God and attempted to obey His many religious laws governing all aspects of their lives. In the synagogue couples were married under a silken canopy, many never having met until the day of the ceremony. Children were born and the boys were circumcised.

The Yiddish language, a mixture of high German, Hebrew, Russian and Polish, was their spoken tongue. Apart from the Sabbath and annual festivals when all work was forbidden, the Jews laboured in their cramped workshops or peddled their wares from stalls in the marketplace. They were buried as instructed by religious edict in the simplest of wooden coffins, the men in their prayer shawls and phylacteries. Then for seven days, their families grieved and prayed while relatives and friends visited the house of mourning to comfort them.

Into such an environment, in the town of Slonim, Michael Marks was born. Slonim lay 620 miles southwest of the imperial capital St Petersburg. It was located in the province of Grodno, towards the north of the Pale of Settlement and on the edge of a wooded plateau at the confluence of two rivers, the Sczava and the Issy.

His date of birth is uncertain. Michael quoted 1859 on his British naturalization papers, yet his wedding certificate implies a date of 1864, while Simon would later quote 1863 as his father's year of birth. His mother Rebecca died shortly after his birth and he was brought up by an elder sister. He would have received a religious education in one of Slonim's many Hebrew schools, culminating in his bar mitzvah in the synagogue at the age of thirteen. His father Mordechai was a tailor, who also owned an interest in a water-powered grain mill in a nearby village. A photograph of Mordechai taken late in life shows a heavily built man with a luxuriant white beard, staring at the camera and wearing on his head the yarmulke or skullcap of the Orthodox Jew. Simon would later recall that his grandfather lived to over a hundred, dying shortly after his son Michael. Apart from Michael, their youngest, Mordechai and Rebecca had four other children: two sons, Barnett and Ephraim, and two daughters, Malke Beile and Esther. All five children would eventually emigrate to the United States or Great Britain.

Mordechai Marks, Michael's father, a tailor in Slonim and part owner of a local grain mill.

The market, Slonim. It is possible that Michael Marks traded here before he left for England in the early 1880s.

Virtually nothing is known of the Marks family history prior to Mordechai's generation. Such slim evidence that exists suggests that the family had for several generations lived either in Slonim town or in one of the surrounding villages. Slonim, in the second half of the nineteenth century, was a typical Russian provincial town. It was a small but significant commercial centre where factories in and around the town produced bricks, tiles, pottery and tar. Local breweries and a distillery manufactured the beer and vodka required by the locals and the soldiers stationed at the nearby regimental and gendarmerie headquarters. Numerous places of worship catered for the town's Jewish, Catholic and Muslim populations.

In the quarter mile which separated the main Orthodox church, adorned with traditional onion-shaped domes, from the similarly imposing seventeenth-century synagogue, lay the town's open marketplace and covered bazaar which accommodated 150 small shops. A contemporary observer described the bazaar as 'a dirty and scruffy ramshackle building with a porch and tiled roof three times higher than the building itself'. It was probably here, in a dingy shop, one of many similar units in the run-down bazaar, that Michael Marks first laid out his wares for sale, trying to make his displays sufficiently attractive to entice roubles and kopecks from the pockets of his Russian peasant and Jewish customers.

Then, quite suddenly, came an event that was to devastate the lives of Michael, his family and his fellow Jews throughout the Russian Empire. On Sunday 13 March 1881, Tsar Alexander II – ironically one of the more liberal rulers in the long line of Romanov tsars – was killed by an assassin's bomb as he drove in his carriage through the snow-covered streets of St Petersburg to the nearby Winter Palace. Among the conspirators (soon captured by the authorities) was a Jewish woman, Hessia Helfman. The tsarist newspapers were soon trumpeting stories of a Jewish conspiracy, and the mood of the mob was fanned into violence. While the local authorities passively looked on, a series of pogroms was activated in the Ukraine and southern Russia. Hundreds of Jews were murdered and injured and their homes burnt out.

The Marks's family home in Slonim may have been one of the 900 homes burnt out in the town in 1881, the year of Alexander's death. It did not take much imagination on the part of Michael and his family to realize that times were bad and would doubtless grow far worse. In fact, the new tsar Alexander III's senior counsellor Constantine Pobedonostsev would later declare that conditions should be made so grim for the Jews that 'one third of the Jews in Russia will emigrate, one third will be forced to accept Baptism and the remainder will starve to death.'

Many Jews decided to leave Russia and seek a safer life abroad; among the first wave of emigrants were Michael and his brother Barnett. The refugees would have set out for one of the north European ports where shipping lines competed for the lucrative immigrant trade. Emigrants were a most welcome replacement cargo for the west-bound ships which had just unloaded their bulk grain cargoes from North America in Bremen, Hamburg or Rotterdam.

Michael would probably have travelled by rail from Slonim via Bialystok and Warsaw to the edge of his known world, the Russian–East Prussian border. Here on the River Vistula, at the border town of Thorn, he might have paused and considered – should he go on to England, a country whose language he could not speak and where he knew no-one apart from his brother? Would he be able to earn a living? Where would he live? He knew that the British Queen Victoria apparently tolerated Jews, but sovereigns die and attitudes change . . . . It was still not too late to return home! He had enough money for the train journey back to his family in Slonim, where perhaps the persecution and harassment would eventually die down and enable him to reopen his little shop in Slonim's bazaar, close to the old synagogue and the cemetery where his mother lay buried.

Michael would have been even more undecided if he had seen the advertisements placed in the Jewish/Russian press by Jewish organizations outside Russia. Fearing their countries would be unable to cope with the influx of immigrants, they warned prospective travellers that work was not available in the West and that religious observance there was lax. But he pressed on. With an exit permit and a passport he would have been able to cross the border legally, despite the Russian police often turning back immigrants for the slightest discrepancy in their travel documents. If he had been unable to obtain the official paperwork, he might have either slipped through an unguarded section of the frontier or bribed a frontier guard. He would then have headed for Hamburg, a major departure port for Britain. And from Hamburg, on board a ship bound for London, the young Michael Marks, a Chaplinesque figure clutching a single piece of luggage containing his worldly possessions, may have peered westwards over the ship's bow as it pitched into the North Sea swell and wondered what fate the Lord had in store for him.

CHAPTER TWO

Come to Manhood

Marks & Spencer Penny Bazaar,
Wakefield, 1890s.

By 1890, when Simon was two years old, his father's business had expanded from a single stall in Leeds's Kirkgate Market to sites in at least five other towns in the north of England including Birkenhead, Castleford, Chesterfield, Wakefield and Warrington. Three could be managed from Leeds, but travelling to Warrington and Birkenhead was more of a problem, as were the potential sites to the north and west of Manchester for new Penny Bazaars which Michael was considering.

He was now having to hire staff in the towns that he found difficult to reach, even when their market days differed from Leeds. In Chesterfield the transport situation brought a problem with the Markets Committee when a Mr Mason, a local trader, complained that Mr Marks had, contrary to market rules, sub-let his stall. Michael had to appear before the Alderman and Councillors of the committee on 2 October 1888 to explain that 'the person selling at his stall at the Market was in his employ'. The local worthies accepted his word and minuted that 'his tenancy of the stall be continued'.

Despite this victory, Michael realized that Leeds was no longer central to his activities and that he would have to seek a new town as his headquarters. There was, however, perhaps a more pressing reason for leaving Leeds. The Leylands district, apart from being home to the majority of newly arrived Jews, was also, in the words of a contemporary writer, 'a hotbed of drunkenness and immorality, the haunt of criminals. Peaceful citizens lived in terror.' On one occasion a police station in the Leylands was raided in broad daylight by a 'gang of roughs and desperados' and the sole occupant, a police inspector, nearly killed. Inevitably the violence affected the Jewish community. They were taunted and molested in the streets, the windows and doors of their homes were daubed and smashed and the synagogues desecrated. For the immigrants, such hostility must have brought back fearful memories of the violence they had only recently left behind in Eastern Europe.

For Michael and Hannah, the safety of their young son Simon, as well as a second child, Rebecca, who had been born in 1890, was paramount. So, in September 1890, the family moved to Wigan, an industrial town of 55,000 people lying twenty miles west of Manchester. Living conditions here were among the worst in Victorian Britain, and the pitheads and shafts of the mining industry extended even to the centre of the town. But, as Goronwy Rees noted in *St Michael – The History of Marks & Spencer*, the town had its advantages: 'Its market was the oldest and largest in Lancashire and its working-class population was of the type to which his [Michael Marks] Penny Bazaars had the strongest appeal. It was also within half an hour's journey by rail to Warrington and Birkenhead and other Lancashire towns like Bolton, which offered a promising field for expansion.'

The Marks's home was a two-up, two-down terrace house at 152 Great George Street, which they rented from Sarah and Anne Dawber for £9 a year. Sixty years later Simon wrote of this house:

'. . . my first memory is of a little house in Wigan at the age of four. The patter of

A studio photograph of Simon; he developed an interest in cricket from an early age, encouraged by Thomas Spencer.

the clogs on the cobbled stoned streets appealed to me enormously and I begged my father to buy me a pair, just like the other children. At night I would wrap them up in brown paper and put them under my pillow. I didn't want to be different from the other children. We lived in modest though comfortable circumstances and conditions, and our happiest times seemed to be when father spent the Sunday with us. He was the most lovable of persons and seemed to be away a great deal. He was of course pre-occupied with the building up of his business to which he devoted all of his energies.'

A Mr Tarshish supplied the furniture for the house on hire purchase at the rate of two shillings and sixpence a week. Within weeks of Michael's arrival in Wigan, he had set up a new stall in the town's Market Hall and rented a second property for use as a warehouse.

On 1 February 1892 a third child, Miriam, was born to Michael and Hannah. Miriam's birth certificate indicates that although ten years had now passed since Michael had arrived in England, he was still unable to sign his name; he had simply penned a cross, which the registrar had qualified as 'The mark of Michael Marks, father'. Michael's occupation was listed as 'Smallware dealer (Master)'.

It was at this time that an event occurred which would put an end to Michael's policy of trading from stalls in open markets. He had rented a stall in Birkenhead's Open Casual Market and had engaged a local girl as a sales assistant. Owing to the market's exposed site and a spell of viciously cold weather, the young lady contracted pneumonia and subsequently died. Michael was devastated and would thenceforth never trade in open markets but only in covered market halls, arcades or high street sites. During this period the four-year-old Simon and his two sisters were being brought up in a homely but not particularly religious environment, as Wigan had few Jewish inhabitants and no synagogue.

As Michael opened more stalls between Liverpool and Manchester, the idea of having the latter as the centre of his activities grew ever more attractive. He may have heard that the anti-Jewish violence in the Leylands area of Leeds had subsided, due in no small way to the community setting up a self-defence organization. It might now, he considered, be safe to move to a city with a larger and more conspicuous Jewish community. By April 1892, when the Marks family moved to a larger house at 57 Darlington Street, Wigan, at double their previous rent, Michael had made up his mind to move to Manchester. However, due to pressure of work his departure was delayed for eighteen months simply because he could not spare the time to look for a suitable new home there.

He was beginning to realize that running a geographically spread business, including a central warehouse and full- and part-time staff, was more than one man could handle on top of his domestic responsibility as father to a growing family. He needed a partner, someone he could trust, who knew the basics of selling, and who could contribute some capital to his growing enterprise. Market traders had previously approached him with offers of a partnership but Michael had always turned them down. He had at one time offered a partnership to a Mr Cook, a Wigan market dealer, who had helped him finance the installation of gas lighting on his stall. To Mr Cook's eternal regret in later years, he refused the offer.

Michael's first serious choice of a partner was Isaac Dewhirst, the wholesaler who had given him credit eight years previously. 'What better than a wholesaler and retailer in partnership?' Michael Marks had asked Mr Dewhirst. Isaac Dewhirst thought otherwise, his warehouse required all his attention; but he suggested Michael consider contacting Tom Spencer, Dewhirst's cashier, who he thought was considering setting up his own business. Tom Spencer was a big, bluff Yorkshireman, eight years Michael's senior. His forebears had lived for at least 200 years in the market town of Skipton, where he was born in 1851 in a house near the high street, a site today occupied by the local branch of Woolworth. Spencer was a heavy drinker, and his fondness for strong liquor may have been the reason for his several changes of employment before settling down as a salesman with I. J. Dewhirst around the time Michael was making his first purchases from the firm.

Over the years, Michael had come to appreciate Tom's administrative abilities at Dewhirst, and his tough – though fair – skill in handling staff. He was also aware that

Thomas Spencer, the bluff Yorkshireman who in 1894 became Michael Marks's partner with an investment of £300.

Spencer was essentially a 'details' man, and was more at home at the warehouse sorting out administrative problems than travelling around the country as Michael did, visiting stores, buying merchandise, seeking new sites and generally probing the retail scene. Tom also had a thrifty side to his nature and insisted on re-using old nails and string at the warehouse rather than buying new. Nevertheless the two men were to work well together and their partnership would prove successful on both a professional and personal level. Simon, too, was very fond of this rotund, good-natured Yorkshireman, who in later years would share his enjoyment of cricket with young Simon and Simon's friend, Israel Sieff, by taking them to matches at Old Trafford. Although at this time he lived in Manchester, Spencer was a staunch supporter of Yorkshire and an expert on the team's players and statistics.

Tom's second wife Agnes had taught at a village school before their marriage. The

A painting of Cheetham Hill Road, Manchester, at the turn of the century, with the domed Great Synagogue on the left. The Marks family lived at No. 20, at the far end of the road beyond the church.

couple met when she visited Dewhirst's to buy Sunday School prizes for her pupils. She was a capable teacher and decided she would assist Michael Marks, her husband's future business partner, in improving his English. She later recalled Michael's delight when, under her supervision, he completed his first cheque in English. In September 1894, Michael, Hannah and their three children moved from Wigan to Manchester, the same month as Tom Spencer bought a half partnership in Michael Marks's business with his life savings of £300.

To the six-year-old Simon, the family's first home at 20 Cheetham Hill Road, a shop with rooms above, was warm and comfortable and established his lifelong love for the city he would later regard as '. . . my home town. It is here that I spent the formative years of my life, where I married, and where I helped to lay the foundations of a new Marks & Spencer.' As a child he would have been unaware that his end-of-terrace home was situated in a most run down and polluted area of the city. Built just north of the city centre on an embankment which overlooked the railway tracks entering Victoria Station, one of the busiest in England, the Marks's home would have been inundated day and night with the sounds and smells of smoke-belching locomotives passing within fifty yards of the back door. Similarly the River Irk, a dark, evil-smelling stream, flowed virtually under the house. Rattling and clanging trams passed the front door, while on the far pavement facing the house was the forbidding entrance to the local workhouse.

In a yard at the rear of the premises Michael stored his goods under tarpaulins, and in the little shop on the ground floor, reached from pavement level by two stone steps, he opened the first Marks & Spencer store – in reality a converted front room. Over the front door and on the window was inscribed 'Marks & Spencer Penny Bazaar', and to encourage customers to come in, the narrow fascia was painted with the words 'Admission Free', on the basis of 'The more they can see, the more they will buy.' This contrasted radically with other shops, where customers came in to buy specific items. For instance, if gloves were required then a selection of gloves would be produced by the sales assistant from under the counter and individually presented to the customer. Browsing was rarely encouraged.

Young Simon may not have noticed the dingy surroundings or wondered why his father, now the part owner of a thriving business, should still be living in one of the poorest areas of Manchester while similarly successful Jewish businessmen were beginning to buy or rent homes along the northern reaches of Cheetham Hill Road and Bury New Road. The reason would not have been personal meanness, for Michael was a most generous man and made weekly visits to the Jewish Working Men's Club, where he would distribute money to the poorest and most needy members.

The likely explanation for Michael and his family living in such poor conditions was that the sheer amount of work, both physical and mental, that he was devoting to the business was affecting his health. The strain of carving out a niche for himself within the tough world of market trading, plus a growing addiction to cheap, pungent cigars which gave him a persistent hacking cough, made Michael realize that it might be well to consider plans for the security of his family. It would, he may well have reasoned, be better to sink his profits back into the business rather than spend the money on a grander house. That way if he should die, his family would have the profits of a thriving business to rely upon for security.

Simon was by now, in 1894, attending the Manchester Jews School, which was situated in Derby Street, just off the main Cheetham Hill Road and a few hundred yards from his home. The school itself was relatively new, having been built in 1869 to accommodate the children of immigrants settling in the Manchester area. The curriculum was basically non-religious, and the essence of the school, with its separate sections for boys and girls, was to convert young East European immigrants or sons and daughters of immigrants into English men and women. Although religious instruction formed a small proportion of the syllabus, additional tuition was received outside school hours at one of the many *cheders* (Hebrew for 'room') or religious schools that proliferated in Jewish communities and operated in the evenings and on Sunday mornings. Emphasis in Simon's school was placed on the English language, culture, games and songs. The use of Yiddish, the sole language spoken in many of the pupils' homes, was strongly discouraged.

This process of anglicization was supported by the elite Anglo-Jewish community who had settled in Manchester well before the arrival of the 'Ost-Juden' or Eastern European Jews from Russia and Poland. Concerned with the anti-Jewish feeling that might be stirred up by the arrival of this army of immigrants, so alien in language and appearance to native Englishmen, they set about introducing the newcomers to the English way of

Simon with his sisters (left to right) Rebecca, Mathilda and Miriam. His fourth sister, Elaine, was born when Simon was fourteen.

life. Similarly, the formation of English-style organizations such as the Jewish Lads Brigade was also encouraged.

The problem of the absorption of the immigrants was felt not only in Manchester but in many other British cities. The *Jewish Chronicle*, in its issue of 12 August 1881, claimed that the newcomers, mainly from Poland, were 'bringing that country into Britain' and were forming a community within a community. The newspaper declared:

> 'This is most undesirable, it is more than a misfortune, it is a calamity. We cannot afford to let them [the newcomers] slide. Our outside world is not capable of making minute discrimination between Jew and Jew and forms its opinion of Jews in general as much, if not more, from them than from the anglicized portion of the community. We are responsible for them.'

The *Jewish Chronicle* obviously reflected the views of the Jewish establishment, some of whose members were descended from the original Sephardic or Spanish and Portuguese Jewish families who had been readmitted into England by Oliver Cromwell in 1656, over three and a half centuries after their original expulsion by King Edward I in 1290. These original families, plus Ashkenazi Jews originating mainly from Germany, had by the time of the arrival of the Russian Polish Jews at the end of the nineteenth century submerged themselves into British society and culture while still maintaining their religious identity. Mainly engaged in the professions and commerce, they had campaigned in previous years, with the aid of Gentile sympathizers, to remove from the British statute book the various discriminatory clauses barring Jews from enjoying complete parity with their Christian neighbours. They were successful, and gradually the barriers fell. In 1833 the first professing Jew was called to the Bar; in 1858 Lionel Rothschild became the first Jewish Member of Parliament and in 1885 his son, Nathaniel Mayer Rothschild, was elevated to the peerage – the first professing Jew to be so honoured. By the time Simon went to school, anglicized Jews were accepted in most sections of society.

The education provided by the Manchester Jews School was sufficient to enable the seven-year-old Simon to write a note to his friends on Christmas Eve 1895. The note, with the linguistic errors of childhood, incidentally indicates the family's move to a more socially acceptable address at 118 Bury New Road and also the birth of Simon's third sister Mathilda, or as he spelt her name 'Mitilder':

118 Bury new Road   Decmember the 24 1895

Dear Freinds on be have fore my mama and My sisters Rebecky Mary and baby Mitilder and Myself we all wish you a Merry Chrismas and a happy new year when it comes we dont only wish for Chrismas and new year but we wish you happnes all the year round your little Jewish freinds Simon Marks

Written by the young Simon, possibly as a school exercise, the wording already hints at a certain seniority or even proprietorship within the family which would become a major aspect of his character in the coming years. The family of which he would eventually become head would comprise not only his children, sisters and *their* spouses and children, but also the company, which he would dominate as Chairman for nearly half a century.

As a schoolboy Simon was physically slight. He appears in early photographs as less than average in height, with large dark eyes peering at the camera from under heavy eyebrows. His early schooldays were a worry to his mother because,

A letter written by Simon, aged seven, in December 1895. The heading indicates that the family had moved to a new address.

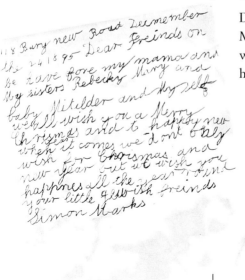

as he wrote years later, 'I always seemed to be in trouble, fighting more or less victoriously with other boys, but whether victorious or not, I always got a further scolding when I returned home, a little dirty with hair dishevelled and my clothes torn with the adventures of the day.'

Another worry for his mother was Simon's religious education. She insisted on his attending the Friday night and Saturday morning synagogue services with a certain degree of guilt, for she knew her husband could not accompany the boy at these times as they were his busiest trading periods of the week. In fact Michael only attended services during the High Holidays, a period which included Rosh Hashanah – the new year – and the solemn fast day of Yom Kippur, the Day of Atonement.

The services were conducted in Hebrew, a language which bears no relationship to English in either its spoken or written form – the script for instance is written from right to left and often omits all vowels – and which required specialist tuition. Simon attended private lessons, but as he commented in later years his tutor was not too well versed in the language, resulting in Simon's being able to *read* the language but virtually unable to understand a word of it. Nevertheless, on the Saturday closest to Simon's thirteenth birthday, 9 July 1901, and in the presence of his family and the congregation of one of Manchester's elite synagogues, Simon read aloud in Hebrew a portion of the Five Books of Moses from a hand-scripted Scroll of the Law. At the conclusion of his bar mitzvah and amid the congregation's shouts of 'Mazal Tov' (Congratulations!), Simon would in religious terms have shed his childhood and become a man.

The first six female staff to be employed in Marks & Spencer Penny Bazaars, photographed c. 1897. From left to right: Ada Probert, Laura Cowburn, Esther Brown, Cissie Rowland, Hilda Cartwright and Gertrude Proctor.

Soon after this event the Marks family moved yet again, this time to a terraced property in the higher reaches of Cheetham Hill Road. (Incidentally this property still stands and was, in 1990, the only one of Michael Marks's various Manchester residences to have survived.) There was a steep flight of stone steps leading from the pavement up to an arched doorway, and behind that wooden stairs leading to the upper floor. From the retailing point of view the most important feature was the basement which occupied a complete floor and could be reached from street level via a door at the front of the building. Here Mr Marks and Mr Spencer stored the merchandise they could not hold in their already overflowing leased warehouse in nearby Robert Street.

By the turn of the century the Robert Street warehouse was servicing the requirements of thirty-six Penny Bazaars situated not only in the Midlands and the north of England but as far south as London and south Wales. Goods were received in the basement via ramps from pavement level – nearly a century later the words 'Marks & Spencer' can still be made out on the lintels over the ramp doors. Teams of workers would then redistribute the goods to the bazaars via railway or horse transport, an operation supervised by Tom Spencer, who shared an office on the second floor with Michael Marks. It soon became apparent that a new warehouse was required to replace the rapidly overstretched Robert Street, and shortly afterwards Simon was able to point out to his school friends with pride the new, purpose-built warehouse, with a near-100-foot frontage, that his father was having built virtually opposite Simon's school in Derby Street.

The Derby Street warehouse that was also the company's registered office from 1903 to 1924.

The Marks family – Michael, Hannah, Simon, Rebecca, Miriam and Mathilda – were soon on the move once again. For a prosperous and wealthy man to live over his stock in Cheetham Hill Road, even the northerly part, was not acceptable to Hannah Marks. Having gathered in the pennies on their first stall in Leeds, working until after midnight preparing merchandise for the next day's trading, she thought she deserved some reward. What could be better, she asked Michael, than a fine house in Bury New Road? The road was in a most respectable area – Higher Broughton in the Borough of Salford. Michael would have been content to remain in Cheetham Hill Road but there were certain factors to consider. 'After all,' he thought, 'Simon was growing up and wanted to entertain his friends in pleasant surroundings. And the girls, in a few years' time, would be bringing their husbands to visit on Friday nights. Perhaps Hannah is right!'

The family found an available house at 396 Bury New Road, but it was not quite to their liking. With uncharacteristic extravagance Michael ordered the existing building to be demolished and constructed a new house, complete with eight bedrooms, a garden summer house, and a large drawing room which, according to an early visitor, contained furniture of rather tasteless design, a piano, some excellent china and a collection of stuffed birds displayed under glass covers. The house also had live-in accommodation for a cook and a maid and was fitted with the status symbols of the period, namely a telephone and a name – 'Knoll House'. Of greater significance to Simon was the fact that his new friend Israel Sieff lived just six houses and fifty yards down the road at Number 408.

The Sieffs had moved in to their home – a terraced property, smaller and less ostentatious than the Marks's – a few weeks before the arrival of Michael and his family. Ephraim Sieff, the head of the household, came from a similar background to Michael Marks. Born in Lithuania, within the Pale of Settlement, he had escaped as a young man by crossing the Russian border in a horsedrawn wagon, hiding under sacks of corn. He landed on Britain's east coast at Hull, and subsequently started a business selling artificial jewellery from a tray in the streets – his pedlar's licence is still in existence. He soon made his way to Manchester, where he laid the basis of his fortune by selling fabric cuttings collected from the floors of tailoring workshops.

On his arrival in Bury New Road, Ephraim Sieff was already a wealthy man. In Manchester he had met and married his wife, also an immigrant from Lithuania, and by 1901 they had four children – Israel, at twelve years the oldest, followed by Pauline, Miriam and William. A fifth child, Edward, would be born in 1905. Israel and Edward were eventually to follow Simon as chairmen of Marks & Spencer.

The first contact between the Marks and Sieff families had occurred just prior to their move to Bury New Road. Young Israel Sieff was walking along Cheetham Hill Road on a bitterly cold Saturday morning when he saw three girls identically dressed in fur-trimmed heavy wool coats. In particular he noticed the pretty legs of the tallest; as he later wrote in his memoirs:

> 'It was the first time I had noticed the shape of a girl's legs. I wanted to see if she had the kind of face I felt instinctively without instruction should go with the legs. So I quickened my pace, got ahead of them and looked back. They were obviously three sisters who were well looked after for they were neat, well shod, trim, belonging to a careful mother who liked to see her children turned out well. The face of the eldest was what I had hoped and expected to see; that is to say it was extremely pretty.'

ABOVE An invitation, printed on pink paper, to the wedding of Ephraim Sieff and Sarah Saffer in 1888. Their eldest son Israel was later to become Simon's lifelong companion and business associate.

RIGHT Rebecca (left), Miriam and Mathilda Marks, who one day caught the eye of the twelve-year-old Israel Sieff when out walking in Cheetham Hill Road. Israel was particularly attracted to Rebecca; the pair became childhood sweethearts and later married.

Israel did not yet know that the pretty girl who caught his eye was Rebecca (or Becky) Marks, Simon's oldest sister. The manners of the time precluded him from talking to the girls, but he noted the number of the house they entered and learned further details of the family from a school friend. A week later Israel met Becky again at a children's party and a few days later Israel Sieff was introduced to Simon Marks at the Marks's home.

Israel's first impression of Simon was '. . . of a dark, eager, vital, forceful boy, altogether

Simon's class at Manchester Grammar School, c. 1903. Simon is in the front row, far right, and Israel in the back row, second from right.

quicker in his speech, gestures and movements than myself. We were as animals very different, which was perhaps why we hit it off.' And hit it off they did. For nearly two-thirds of a century the two men were friends, partners, colleagues and brothers-in-law – each marrying the other's sister. Their 'David and Jonathan' relationship ended only with Simon's death in 1964. Israel would always maintain that Simon was the senior partner in their relationship: 'All through it he [Simon] remained the one who possessed the bat, ball and wickets, and I was happy and fulfilled under his captaincy.' Israel was a man of great intellect and ability, and his lifelong lieutenancy to Simon perhaps reflected his realization that immense influence can often be effectively exercised from a position once removed from the very top.

Simon's youngest sister Elaine was born at the family's new home in 1902, an event witnessed by Israel Sieff as he accidentally barged into Mrs Marks's room at the moment

Two pages of Michael Marks's application for naturalization (1897), giving his occupation as 'general dealer'. By this time he had learned to sign his name in English.

of delivery while searching for his friend Simon. A few months earlier, in September 1901, Simon had begun his secondary education. His father Michael had taken much time and counsel from family and friends before deciding on his son's future school. Michael's brother Ephraim had arrived in England in 1890, following national service in the tsar's army; he was religiously very observant and might have suggested a career as a rabbi for his young nephew.

But Simon's parents thought otherwise. They considered Simon, although only thirteen years of age, to be his father's natural successor to manage the family interest in Marks & Spencer. The company was expanding and would need a capable man at its head – capable not only in business terms but well educated, particularly in modern languages, as many of the company's suppliers were now located in Germany and France. Moreover, as Michael and Hannah were only too well aware, any future chairman of the company might eventually have to shoulder the responsibilities of the Spencer side of the business; Tom Spencer's heavy drinking was affecting his health and his son, Tom Junior, though still in his teens, was also developing a taste for alcohol. The search for a school to provide the education for a future company chairman soon narrowed to a single candidate – the Manchester Grammar School.

Founded in 1515, the school had over the centuries gained a fine reputation for scholastic achievement. In 1895, a report to the Royal Commission on Secondary Education had stated that the 'extraordinary number of boys which it [the school] sends up annually to the Universities', plus other attributes, 'give it a foremost and in some respect *the* foremost place amongst the great day schools of England.' The school had other advantages besides in the eyes of Simon's parents. Firstly – and unusually – there was no apparent bias against Jewish children, the first having attended the school in 1827. This liberal policy was confirmed in 1879 when the High Master, Mr Dill, declared that the school was 'open to all classes and creeds in the Kingdom'.

To Michael Marks the school represented the educational opportunities he had missed as a boy in Russia. From his first Manchester home at the foot of Cheetham Hill Road Michael could watch the Manchester Grammar School pupils make their way from the railway station to the school's entrance in Long Millgate between the station and the cathedral. Such was the school's reputation that pupils would daily travel up to thirty miles from the towns and villages around Manchester to attend it. Simon did not have to travel such a distance; from Knoll House to the school's Victorian Gothic entrance over which was inscribed 'SCHOLA MANCUNIENSIS 1870' was about two miles, a short journey on the horsedrawn buses that trundled along Bury New Road into the heart of the city.

Israel Sieff had joined the school three months earlier than Simon, at the beginning of the mid-summer term 1901. He would collect his friend every morning for their journey to school. Simon, years later recalled his first day: ' . . . entering the portals of the old building in Long Millgate, I was overawed by the gowned masters and by the formidable prefects. I was overawed by its overpowering atmosphere which I realize now was the mystique which lay hidden within its grey walls.'

For Michael, his son's entry into the school was a further step in the family's anglicization. Four years earlier he had applied for and received British nationality. His application indicated his gratitude to the country that had granted him shelter and the opportunity to set up a home and a business. It was also legally easier to do business in Britain if you were British. The protection afforded by British citizenship during the numerous business trips he was now making abroad was a major consideration.

The citizen who acquires his nationality through official application rather than by accident of birth must have his character officially recorded and registered for approval by the authorities. In Michael's case the authority required was that of the Right Honourable Sir Mather White Ridley, Her Majesty's Principal Secretary of State for the Home Department. Michael's reputation as a decent, hardworking man was therefore confirmed in writing first by the mayor of Wigan, Robert Richards, who wrote of Michael that he was 'reported to have been respectable and of good character whilst resident in Wigan'. Inspector Jackson of the Chief Constable's office, Town Hall, Manchester, similarly reported that Mr Marks was 'a respectable man and his statements are true'.

If Michael's primary objective in sending Simon to the Grammar School was to produce an Englishman able to speak and write in French and German, then he was successful. As Simon moved up through the forms his scholastic record improved and he consistently achieved high placings, including 'top of the form' in both languages, reasonably high marks in mathematics, but only average in science and drawing. He also learned to appreciate, as he later recalled, those subjects such as literature and poetry which in the words of Hugh Oldham, the school's founder, 'contributed to good learning and manners'. Poetry and literature in the languages of Shakespeare, Goethe and Molière, Simon later mused, was not a bad foundation for adult life.

Michael Marks's favourite store at 60 Oldham Street, Manchester, photographed in 1898.

Sport was then considered of great importance in the development of a young man's character, and on the school's campus was a gymnasium sufficiently large to accommodate the physical exertions of up to 500 boys at any one time. The gymnasium contained a boxing ring, but Simon's sole venture into the sport ended abruptly when he bloodied the nose of his sparring partner – Israel. Both friends found the experience so traumatic they never again donned boxing gloves. Simon was especially keen on cricket and played regularly for the school's second team. On three occasions he played for the first eleven, recording a run score of zero, one, zero. 'The remarkable thing about this average is that it is 0.33 recurring and still recurring to my dismay,' Simon later ruefully observed.

For much of his four years at MGS, Simon was in the same forms as Israel Sieff. Their ability to communicate with each other on an almost telepathic basis was becoming apparent. If Simon made a mistake in his homework the chances were that Israel would make an identical error. Simon on one occasion left his homework at home and the next morning apologized to the class. The master of the sixth, Mr Horsely, interjected with 'Don't worry, Marks. I shall know exactly how to mark you as I have Sieff's exercise.' The records that survive indicate that whenever Simon and Israel sat the same examinations Simon would usually get higher marks than his friend. This disparity perhaps explains Simon's genuine envy of Israel's university education and the economics degree he acquired at Manchester University. Simon, on the other hand, with a higher scholastic record, was dispatched to the Continent after his final years at MGS, to improve his French and German. Later in life he would always hold in high regard anyone who had got a degree.

Israel, it must be noted, had not wished to go up to university but would have preferred immediately to join Sieff and Beaumont, his father's fabric business. Ephraim however insisted that his son should study for a degree. Israel's remark that his father had built up a successful business without a degree was met by Ephraim's unanswerable retort, 'Do you know what kind of business I would have if I had a degree?'. Simon would eventually achieve academic recognition in 1939, when he was awarded an honorary Doctor of Science degree by London University. 'Now I am level with Israel' he said after the ceremony.

Simon was to look back on his days at Manchester Grammar School with great affection. He showed this in practical terms by donating considerable sums of money towards the development of the school, including £50,000 in 1962 for the construction of a science wing. Israel similarly gave generously to the school and took his affection a step further when he incorporated the school's owl emblem into his personal coat of arms when he was elevated to the peerage in 1966.

While Simon was enjoying his final years at MGS, important developments were taking place at Marks & Spencer. In 1903 the company comprised forty bazaars in high streets and market halls around the country and had made a profit of £7,000. Mr Marks and Mr Spencer realized that their partnership – which had previously managed the company on a successful, albeit 'back of an envelope' basis – now needed a more permanent and stable arrangement.

Both men were in their middle years, and both their families and their staff, who now numbered well over 200, needed reassurance that the company would survive if either partner, for whatever reason, left the company. So in 1903 a private company, Marks and Spencer Limited, was registered with a capital of 30,000 £1 shares. Each partner received 14,995 shares and of the balance of ten shares, seven were allocated one each to the seven subscribers to the Memorandum and Articles of Association. The remaining three shares were not issued until 1906.

The new arrangement, assuming that Mr Marks and Mr Spencer continued to work together in harmony, ensured that control of the company would remain in their hands. However, if the two partners or those who subsequently replaced them should disagree, control of the company could pass to the owners of the few loose shares. This was to occur later, creating grave difficulties for Simon.

In 1903, however, these problems were not apparent and the company seemed destined

A page of the Articles of Association of Marks and Spencer Ltd, 1903. The signatures include those of Michael Marks and Thomas Spencer.

The Marks & Spencer stall in Norfolk Market Hall, Sheffield, which opened in 1897.

to continue its relentless progress. Virtually everything displayed in the bazaars was still being sold under the banner 'Don't Ask the Price, it's a Penny'. The range of goods consisted of hundreds of different items such as cotton reels, collar studs, labels and so on, as well as more substantial articles including padlocks, screwdrivers, nutmeg graters, crockery and dolls. To keep his customers satisfied, Michael was forever searching for new lines to replace older and slower selling ones. The public expected, even for a penny, to see new items on display whenever they visited their local 'Marks & Sparks' bazaar.

While Michael enjoyed the selection, buying and bargaining, the pressure on him as

RIGHT ABOVE Examples of typical Penny Bazaar merchandise.

RIGHT BELOW Early examples of Marks & Spencer sheet music. During this period, many households would have owned a piano, and at a penny a sheet these songs and piano pieces were very popular for home entertainment.

the business progressed was becoming overwhelming. He was working virtually seven days a week. His partner Tom was invaluable on the administrative and distribution side of the business, and had also introduced the concept – to be so successfully exploited by future generations of leaders – of buying direct from the manufacturer. But Tom was not a merchant. He had no true 'feel' for the products the partners sold, and Michael could only rely on him to a very limited extent to buy goods. To add to Michael's problems, one of the reasons for forming the private company was Spencer's decision to retire and take up gentleman farming near the village of Whittington, north of Birmingham. Tom

37

ABOVE Tom and Agnes retired to Whittington Farm in 1903, but Tom continued to attend Marks & Spencer board meetings until his death in 1905.

RIGHT The Spencer family on the steps of Whittington Farm, near Lichfield. Agnes, Tom's second wife, is sitting in front of her husband.

would henceforward regard his company duties solely as attending the monthly board meetings in Manchester and drawing his half of the profits. He enjoyed life with his second wife Agnes, in their comfortable Georgian farmhouse, feeding the chickens, herding the cows, supervising his farm manager and – unfortunately – drinking.

At the age of fifty-three, after only two years of semi-retirement, Tom Spencer died. Michael and Simon attended his funeral at the village church in Whittington and must have wondered, as they stood by the grave, about who would replace Spencer as Michael's partner. Prior to Tom's death, Michael had visited him at his Whittington farmhouse to discuss possible successors. Among the contenders was Tom Junior, Spencer's twenty-three-year-old son, although both Michael and Tom realized that the young man did not have the necessary inclination or business acumen to replace his father. An alternative was Tom's wife Agnes who, although she had the personality and ability to do the job, had virtually no business experience. Isaac Dewhirst, Tom's friend and ex-employer, seemed the most appropriate choice, but when offered the opportunity he again turned it down, as he had eleven years earlier. This second refusal caused Spencer to replace Dewhirst as executor of his will.

William Chapman, the eventual choice, was chairman of a firm of handkerchief manufacturers who supplied Marks & Spencer. Chapman was a tall, fair-haired man, determined in manner and with cold, ruthless eyes that were a true indication of his character as a classic self-made man. Chapman was an illegitimate child, brought up in a street mission in Manchester. As a boy he had sold newspapers outside the Exchange

ABOVE Thomas Spencer Junior was appointed a director of Marks & Spencer in 1911. He died prematurely in 1917, aged thirty-six.

ABOVE RIGHT William Chapman, c. 1910. Chapman was Tom Spencer's executor, and chairman of Marks & Spencer from Michael Marks's death in 1907 until 1916, when Simon won back control for the Marks family.

Street railway station and held the heads of cab horses while the businessmen passengers alighted outside their premises. One of these businessmen was sufficiently impressed by young Chapman's keen manner to offer him a job in his handkerchief factory. Seven years later William Chapman was the company's chairman. Soon his firm was selling goods to Marks & Spencer, at whose Head Office in Derby Street he became friendly with Tom Spencer. With Chapman's subsequent appointment as Spencer's successor, the lines of a future battle for the control of Marks & Spencer had been drawn, a battle in which Chapman's chief opponent would be Simon Marks.

In 1905, however, the year of Spencer's death, Simon was only a seventeen-year-old boy on the verge of leaving school and about to travel to Europe at his father's insistence to complete his education and widen his experience. Though young, the tough, assertive and occasionally arrogant side of his personality was already apparent. At home his sisters respected and perhaps feared him. The exception was Becky, who considered herself a match for any man. Brother and sister often engaged in furious arguments that sometimes ended with them hurling books and plates at each other. In later life Becky's strong will and dynamic personality, which Simon never allowed her to exercise within the confines of Marks & Spencer, would be channelled into the creation of a multitude of good works and charitable institutions. Simon's youngest sister Elaine wrote of her brother, 'He was fourteen when I was born and from the first moment we made contact until my teenage years I was in total awe of him.' And indeed, to Simon, his baby sister was beneath his notice; he once even put her on his lap, tummy down, as a prop for his newspaper.

WHERE would you like best to live? _London_

What are your favorite amusements? _Cricket and football_

What is your ambition? _To have a handle to my name_

What is your idea of happiness? _Speaking to a nice, nice girl_

What is your idea of misery? _To be in bed while the one's cricket team is playing a match_

What is your favorite character in history? _King Alfred_

What historical character do you most dislike? _James I_

What is your favorite character in fiction? _Leonard Holt_

What are your favorite qualities in man? _Tenacity & Straightforwardness_

What are your favorite qualities in woman? _Sympathy & determination_

What are your favorite authors and books? _Dumas "Monte Christo"_

What are your favorite painters and pictures?

What are your favorite actors and plays? _Miss Nora Kerin in "As you like it"_

What are your favorite musical compositions? _Faust & Tannhäuser_

What are your favorite names for men and women? _Noël & Rosa_

What is your favorite flower, color, and perfume? _Rose, red & Eau de Cologne_

What is your favorite food and drink? _Roast Turkey_

What fault have you most toleration for? _Bluntness_

What is your favorite adage or motto? _If at first you don't succeed, try, try, try again_

Signed _Simon Marks_

A questionnaire completed by Simon at the age of sixteen. It was also completed by Israel Sieff and Simon's sisters.

When Simon had passed his sixteenth birthday he completed a questionnaire, perhaps as a party game, listing his favourite and least favourite activities. To the question 'What is your idea of misery?' Simon wrote 'To be in bed while one's cricket team is playing a match.' As for his idea of happiness, he put down 'Speaking to a nice, nice girl'. Against the question requesting his favourite actor or actress, he entered 'Miss Nora Kerin in *As You Like It*'. Simon may have watched the nineteen-year-old actress when she appeared as Rosalind in a performance of the play in Manchester in 1902. He listed his favourite fictional character as Leonard Holt, the hero of *Old St Paul's*, a literary melodrama written by an ex-pupil of the Manchester Grammar School, William Ainsworth, and published in 1841. The book relates the seventeenth-century adventures of a humble grocer's apprentice, who by rescuing his sovereign Charles II from the Great Fire of London is created a lord and finally marries his childhood sweetheart.

Further answers gave Simon's favourite food as roast turkey and his favourite historical character as King Alfred. Personal qualities that Simon favoured included 'tenacity, bluntness and straightforwardness' in men, while in women he preferred 'sympathy and determination'. He summarized these attributes in his favourite motto: 'If at first you don't succeed, try, try, try again.'

Despite his fondness for Manchester, Simon listed London as the place he would prefer to live and his favourite amusements as cricket and football. To the question 'What is your ambition?', he wrote, 'To have a handel [sic] to my name', an aim he was to achieve twice over when he was awarded a knighthood in 1944 and in 1962 a peerage.

At the end of the mid-summer term 1905, Simon left Manchester Grammar School and prepared for his first lengthy spell away from home. With hindsight he wrote that he was 'pleased to have the opportunity of living abroad for three years, learning languages and the way of life of people in other lands'. He was nevertheless extremely nervous when he set off with his father to meet Theodore Guggenheimer, the Marks & Spencer agent in Nuremberg. The company's interest in this historic Bavarian city, situated in the forested uplands of southern Germany, centred on its thriving toymaking industry. German toys were among the finest in the world and found a ready sale in Marks & Spencer's growing chain of Penny Bazaars.

In Nuremberg Simon found lodgings – at thirty shillings per week including breakfast – with a German family whom he later described as 'kindly disposed people in somewhat reduced circumstances'. During the day his father had arranged that he work as a volunteer in J. W. Spear's toy and games factory on the outskirts of the city. In the evenings he either ate alone in restaurants or visited the Guggenheimers, whom he soon came to regard as substitutes for the family he had left in England. Theo Guggenheimer especially appeared in Simon's adolescent eyes as both guardian and guide. Certain matters, however, Simon felt unable to discuss with either Theo or his own parents in Manchester – 'My first book on sex', he wrote years later in some unpublished notes, 'was sent to me by the Bank Manager!' – presumably from England. Simon would repay the Guggenheimers's hospitality in the 1930s, when he made it possible for the family, refugees from Hitler's Germany, to establish themselves in London.

During his period abroad Simon corresponded regularly with Israel Sieff, who was studying at Manchester University; their weekly letters were based on the philosophical letters exchanged between Goethe and Schiller, a correspondence Simon and Israel had studied during their schooldays. The friends kept the letters for many years, sadly destroying them during the Second World War as in Simon's words 'they were jejeune' and gave the impression 'we were flying our kites too high.'

Simon admired Nuremberg as a city, favourably comparing its cleanliness, modern facilities and the civic pride of its residents with Manchester's 'grim and squalid main streets with very few worthwhile buildings'. He enjoyed walking the three-mile circuit of the city's turreted medieval wall, an outing which allowed him to travel back as he put it 'from the twentieth to the sixteenth century'. After the Second World War, Simon reflected on how the city's small Jewish community, apparently well respected by the neighbours at the time of his visit in 1906, had in less than thirty years been hounded by the same neighbours 'into the accursed concentration camps of evil memory'.

In 1906 the eighteen-year-old Simon enjoyed the *gemütlichkeit* of the city and the surrounding Bavarian countryside. He improved his German to what he considered a 'tolerable standard' and joined a '*Tanz-Kurs*' (dance club), where with a group of young people he learned to dance and acquired the social graces necessary to escort his various partners to the theatre and the opera.

Simon, aged seventeen, in fancy dress while staying in Nuremberg where his father had sent him to improve his German.

Meanwhile, in Britain, Marks & Spencer, under the control of Michael Marks and his new partner William Chapman, was progressing well enough to allow, between 1905 and 1907, annual dividends of 20 per cent to be paid on its original capital. Nearly two-thirds of the company's branches were now sited in high streets, a situation which allowed for expansion and development opportunities not possible with the older, inflexible arcade or market hall units. The company was poised for even greater progress. But again Michael Marks was left with the major responsibility for managing the expanding business. His partner, though capable and energetic, was giving, not unnaturally, the majority of his time and effort to the operation of his own handkerchief company. In consequence, Michael was working himself literally to death. He considered bringing Simon home

A London County Council tram in Islington, with the Marks & Spencer Penny Bazaar in the background, 1907.

from the Continent to help him with the burden of work but eventually decided to allow his son to complete his term abroad.

As originally planned, Simon therefore took his leave of Nuremberg and set off for Paris. He at once fell in love with the city. 'Paris never seems to sleep', he wrote to Israel Sieff, and related how he walked the boulevards and toured the art galleries, museums, theatres and other attractions of the world's cultural capital. His father gave him an allowance of 225 francs a month, which considering that the rent of his single room plus his food bills amounted to 160 francs did not leave him with much over to enjoy the life of a 'boulevardier'. It was only when he began to earn an extra 100 francs a month at the firm of Alfred Behrens and Company, where his father had arranged for him to undertake his French business training, that Simon had some cash to spare.

The firm, situated in the rue du Faubourg Poissonière, acted as agents for Marks & Spencer, shipping merchandise direct from French manufacturers to Marks & Spencer in Manchester. Simon was fortunate in having an Austrian, a Mr Marschner, as his manager in charge of the English section of Behrens activities. He was therefore able both to practise his French and to sharpen up his German conversation. It was another individual, however, a German friend of Michael Marks named Obendorfer who, on his visits to Paris several times a year on business, took Simon under his wing and introduced the young man to the good life of the capital.

Simon's first months in Paris had been lonely, and he later wrote that he was 'pleased to retire to my bed early so that I could dream of home and be with my parents and sisters.' Nevertheless, fifteen months later, after Simon (with the help of Mr Obendorfer) had in his own words 'begun to acquire a glimmering of an understanding of the "esprit Gaulois" ', his longing for home had disappeared. Indeed, his father had considerable difficulty in persuading him to return to Manchester. But in November 1907 the nineteen-year-old Simon dutifully returned to the family home in familiar, friendly, Bury New Road. His absence from home had, as he later recalled, given him a feeling of independence and taught him 'the ways of the world'.

His father, delighted at the return of his son, arranged for Simon to share his office with him. About two weeks after his return, while Simon was checking some invoices, the company accountant, Mr Kenyon, entered the office. Michael was leaning back in his chair, smoking a cigar and quietly watching his son. Suddenly, Michael turned to the accountant, proudly pointed at Simon and declared 'Mr Kenyon – my Prince'.

By now the company was becoming sufficiently prosperous to attract the attention of other multiple retailers. The managing director of one such organization, Mr Watson of the Maypole Dairy Company, approached Michael with a proposal for a merger, only to receive the tart reply 'I can lose my money myself!' A more agreeable meeting occurred in 1907 in Croydon, South London, when Michael Marks invited John Sainsbury, the founder of the giant food chain, to the opening in the high street of his Penny Bazaar. The site, next to the Sainsbury store, had been purchased from Sainsburys as part of Marks & Spencer's expansion drive into southern England. Simon attended the opening and apparently made a considerable impression on Mr Sainsbury; 'I like your son, Mr Marks,' declared the founder of Sainsbury, ' . . . he will go far.' But these pleasant occasions as Simon was gently introduced into the business by his father were to last but a month or two.

Just prior to Christmas 1907 Michael had a particularly strenuous week. Simon described how his father:

> ' . . . travelled to Glasgow where he had made arrangements for the purchase of chocolates from a firm called Reeves; he had travelled to Cork and back, where he had bought a considerable quantity of tinned milk in penny cans; he had travelled to London and back. He was convinced that he had to enter the food business. "People must eat", he was wont to say.'

On Christmas Eve even Michael could not travel far from home. Instead he took Simon, Tom Spencer Junior and a business friend to lunch at Manchester's Victoria Hotel. Afterwards the party split up, with Michael setting off for his favourite store in nearby

A PENSION IN PARIS
By S. M.

DEAR JOHN BULL,

I promised you some weeks ago that I would write you more fully about my life and doings in Paris, which must, I know, interest you from different points of view, and not the least from the psychological point of view, which every such keen student of human nature as you appreciate more than any other.

A Pension in Paris corresponds to a London boarding-house. The mere name is unpoetical and material to the extreme. But the cosmopolitan nature of a Pension in Paris arouses more than passing interest, and the one I habit is no exception to the cosmopolitan medley, which runs so rife in Paris.

There are about ten pensionnaires or boarders, who sit at the dinner table, and who represent so many different nationalities. The common language, which connects us all, is, of course, French, which is considerably mutilated by all except the natives, and I take rather a pleasure in studying the types of the different nationalities I have before

me and how each comes to live in this Pension.

As is natural, I will commence by the "Maitresse de Pension," a most interesting personality. She was the daughter of a colonel, who had died fighting in the war of 1870, a fact of which she never grows tired of repeating to us. In her younger days her aspirations were aimed at music, and in this she was only partially successful, because of an illness which laid her low for a considerable time. She did not, however, despair, and worked up a connection as a teacher of piano and singing. That she was successful in this is borne out by the fact that she has so many friends around her. Her old illness, however, again getting the upper hand, she had to leave everything and set up a Pension, to which chance has directed my footsteps.

Time has made her a great gossip, and has also abnormally developed her spirit of inquisitiveness. She wishes to know everything about everybody, and nothing less than everything satisfies her, and through this she is continually at cross purposes with her friends.

Part of an article about his life in Paris written by Simon for the *Marks & Spencer's Grand Annual*, 1909–10. Several family members contributed to this short-lived publication.

Mr. Michael Marks, Manchester.

By the death of Mr. Michael Marks, which occurred on December 31, a remarkable figure has been removed from the business life of the community. It is about 20 years since Mr. Michael Marks left Poland and settled here. At that time he was without capital, and his educational advantages had been few indeed. He started in a very small way by selling penny articles at town and country fairs, and in this way—entirely without assistance—he laid the foundation of the remarkable "Penny Bazaar" business which for long has been principally associated with his name. To-day Messrs. Marks and Spencer, Limited, have establishments all over the country. The success of a business of this description depends largely on system, and in every department of the business Mr. Marks introduced strict method. His integrity was of the highest character, and his detestation of a lie or of subterfuge in any form was one of his most strongly marked characteristics. He never attempted to question or repudiate a bargain when once made. The accumulation of wealth did not lead him to abandon his simple tastes, and although he gave very generously to charities, his expenditure upon himself was moderate. Many stories of his generosity are told, and it is said that on one occasion, hearing that an Englishman was being unduly pressed by a Jewish money-lender, he, quite unsolicited, found the necessary money, giving with it the excellent advice that in future money-lenders, both Jewish and Gentile, should be avoided. Some years ago he became a naturalised Englishman, and always bore a strong affection for the country of his adoption. In religion he was a strict Jew, and took an active part in the many excellent Jewish charitable organisations. He was always genial and cheerful, and insisted that all the assistants in the firm's establishments should show a bright and cheerful front. The funeral service was conducted by the Rev. Dr. D. Soloman, the Rev. H. Newman, and the Rev. H. Levin. The burial, on January 2, took place at the Crumpsall Cemetery of the Old Hebrew Congregation. In addition to crowds of Manchester friends many London faces were noticeable, and among others present were Messrs. J. J. Gilbert, J.P., L.C.C., J. D. Kiley, J. Levy, Mr. Davies (Gottschalk, Dreyfus, and Davies), and very many others, as also representatives of the many charities and societies with which Mr. Marks had identified himself. The deceased was only 47 years of age, his death being due to heart failure. Great sympathy will be felt for his wife, and for the son and four daughters whom he leaves.

The late Mr. Michael Marks. The Manchester community has suffered a loss it c[an] afford in the death of Mr. Michael Marks, who has p[assed] away at the age of forty-six. There was not one ins[titu]tion which did not count him as a supporter, and whene[ver] he could assist the poor and needy he was willing to stretch out the ready [hand] of help and succour. He was the originator of the "Penny Bazaar," both [in Manchester] and in the North of England, by which he opened up a new source of [lif]e to hundreds of people. Not only has the Old Hebrew Congregation to [mourn] his loss, but the whole community has expressed its great sorrow at [the de]mise of an upright, well-disposed and kindly member, who, by his [peac]e and large-heartedness to the needy of all denominations, caused [the] Jew to be honoured and respected. His integrity, united with a [purit]y of character and with a peace-seeking and conciliatory [spirit won] on him general respect and love. A great concourse, including [Je]ws and Christians from London and the neighbouring towns, [...] S.

MISCELLANEOUS.

I regret to announce the death of Mr. Michael Marks, of Higher Broughton, who died on Tuesday at the age of 46. Mr. Marks was an earnest supporter of local communal institutions, and a man of great private beneficence also. Great sympathy is felt with his wife and children.

FUNERAL OF MR. M. MARKS.

The funeral of the late Mr. Michael Marks, of the "Penny Bazaar" fame, took place this afternoon at the Crumpsall Cemetery of the old Hebrew Congregation, of which he was a well-known member. Prominent members of the community represented the numerous charities with which Mr. Marks was connected. About 30 or 40 carriages following the cortège. The funeral service was conducted by the Rev. Dr. B. Soloman, Rev. H Newman, Rev. H Levin of the great Synagogue.

Jewish Working Men's Club. Dr. S. Jacob (Leeds) delivered an address last Sunday on "Dickens and his Treatment of the Jew." Dr. J. Dulberg presided. The lecturer read several quotations from Dickens's works.

The Chairman asked the meeting to express their sympathy at the severe loss the club had sustained at the death of the late Michael Marks, who had taken so keen an interest in the club and its various societies. The members rose in silent sympathy.

The third annual dance of the Operatic Society of the Club was held last Saturday at the Derby Hall, Cheetham. There was a good attendance and the dance was a social and financial success. Mr. B. Goldberg was M.C.

Contemporary newspaper notices of Michael Marks's death on 31 December 1907 praising his philanthropy.

Oldham Street, while Simon visited another branch in Stretford Road. Shortly after they parted Michael collapsed in the street. As he fell, he called out his son's name but Simon did not hear. When Michael recovered he was taken home in a taxi. Later that afternoon Simon returned to Bury New Road to find his father confined to bed, with a nurse in attendance.

After three days Simon was allowed in to see his father, whom he wrote later '. . . was in a good humour and spoke at length about his early life. I am sorry to say I have forgotten much of what he told me but he had a happy purposeful life. That night the crisis came. He did not recover consciousness and on the last day of the year 1907 his spirit passed away.' So, still in his forties, Michael Marks died, a simple man and a great merchant, whose highly successful chain of bazaars were the sure foundation on which

PIONEER OF PENNY BAZAARS.

Death of a Generous Manchester Jew.

Photo by Brown, Barnes and Bell, Manchester.

Mr. MICHAEL MARKS,

A prominent member of the Manchester Jewish community, and the pioneer of the "penny bazaar" business, whose death occurred at Broughton yesterday.

Originally started in a very small way—with a stall in the market place in the lesser Lancashire towns—the enterprise grew until it had its headquarters in a palatial warehouse in Cheetham, and shop establishments in all parts of the North of England.

Mr. Marks, who was only 47 years of age, was a man of exceedingly generous disposition. He was a member of the Committee of the Jewish Working Men's Club, and a supporter of the Home for Aged and Needy Jews, the Jewish Hospital, the Talmud Torah School and a leading member of the Old Hebrew Congregation.

As an instance of his open-handedness, and at the same time of his patriotism, it may be mentioned that during the Boer War, when the "Chronicle" fund for the relief of the soldiers' families was running in our columns, Mr. Marks contributed every week the sum of ten shillings under the modest description, "From a Jew." It is also stated by friends that the rents of certain house property which he had bought were religiously set aside by him for benevolent purposes.

Simon would build a great business enterprise. He left nearly £30,000 in his will (equivalent to about £600,000 in 1993) and a legacy of friendship from the many people, Jew and Gentile alike, he had helped over the years. His funeral drew one of the largest attendances ever seen at Manchester's Jewish cemetery.

To Simon the loss of his father was devastating. Just six weeks after his return from the Continent, aged nineteen and with virtually no training or experience, he had become the sole supporter of his mother and four sisters. He later wrote to a friend:

> 'it has been a terrible time to go through. The responsibility which so suddenly descended on me has aged me by ten years. At least that is how I feel. Nothing so ages a man . . . At home everything is different. Everything which used to be so jolly is now dispiriting. We wait for the absentee but he does not come. We speak of him so often but he cannot hear. It is only now that we are beginning to understand what death means, what a terrible chasm separates us.'

As he stood by his father's grave, Simon knew that the halcyon days of his childhood and youth were over. He would, in the words of the *Talmud*, have to 'be a man where there is no man'.

Michael Marks's tombstone. His funeral, on 2 January 1908, drew one of the largest attendances ever seen at Manchester Jewish Cemetery – some thirty to forty carriages followed the cortège.

CHAPTER THREE

A Taste of Power

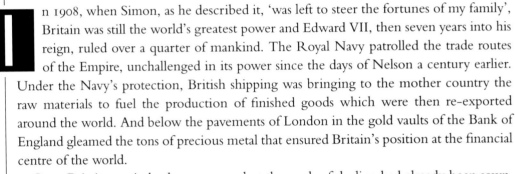

I
n 1908, when Simon, as he described it, 'was left to steer the fortunes of my family', Britain was still the world's greatest power and Edward VII, then seven years into his reign, ruled over a quarter of mankind. The Royal Navy patrolled the trade routes of the Empire, unchallenged in its power since the days of Nelson a century earlier. Under the Navy's protection, British shipping was bringing to the mother country the raw materials to fuel the production of finished goods which were then re-exported around the world. And below the pavements of London in the gold vaults of the Bank of England gleamed the tons of precious metal that ensured Britain's position at the financial centre of the world.

Great Britain was indeed prosperous; but the seeds of decline had already been sown. The South African war had ended in 1902 after the Boer farmers had unexpectedly held off the might of the British Army for nearly three years, clearly indicating deficiencies within Britain's military establishment. Economically, Britain's share of world markets was also declining, while those of her rivals America and Germany were rising.

Unless, however, a person was among the third of Britain's population who lived in poverty due to old age, unemployment, low wages or sickness, life could be very pleasant in Edwardian Britain. Simon was among the fortunate; his late father's resourcefulness and hard work had placed his family within a relatively wealthy segment of the population. This was, however, not immediately apparent to Simon, who later wrote, 'my father had died on the last day of the year, which was also the end of the financial year of the business. The dividends which had accrued were regarded as capital on which Estate Duty had to be paid. There were no liquid funds. My father owned nearly half of the equity of Marks & Spencer. He depended on his dividends.' The Marks family had, therefore, to ' . . . borrow from the bank to live and await the next year's dividends. The future without the pilot looked grim.'

Simon's main concern was for his mother Hannah, who was unable to reconcile herself to her husband's early death. Her bustling and energetic character soon deteriorated into one of gloom and despondency. To add to Simon's domestic problems, there was the health of his epileptic sister Mathilda (Tilly). Her fits and blackouts were unpredictable and as normal schooling was considered out of the question, she was taught by a private governess who visited the house every day. Simon was determined that neither his mother nor his sister would suffer financially from his father's death. It became, as he later recalled, 'an ambition and obsession with me to work for my mother and to try to accumulate a nest egg of £10,000 for her and £5,000 for my sister, Mathilda, who at the time was a sick person and who, I thought, could never achieve independence.' But how was he to amass such large sums of money?

What to him was particularly galling was that the business which had throughout his life been a permanent backcloth to his very existence, was no longer under the direct control of his family. Admittedly, the Marks family owned half the company's equity, but

Teddy Sieff (Israel's younger brother), Mathilda Marks (centre) and Elaine Marks, c. 1908.

OPPOSITE An early company letterhead, black bordered, presumably to mark the recent death of the founder. Simon wrote this letter in German in April 1908, three months after his father's death.

46

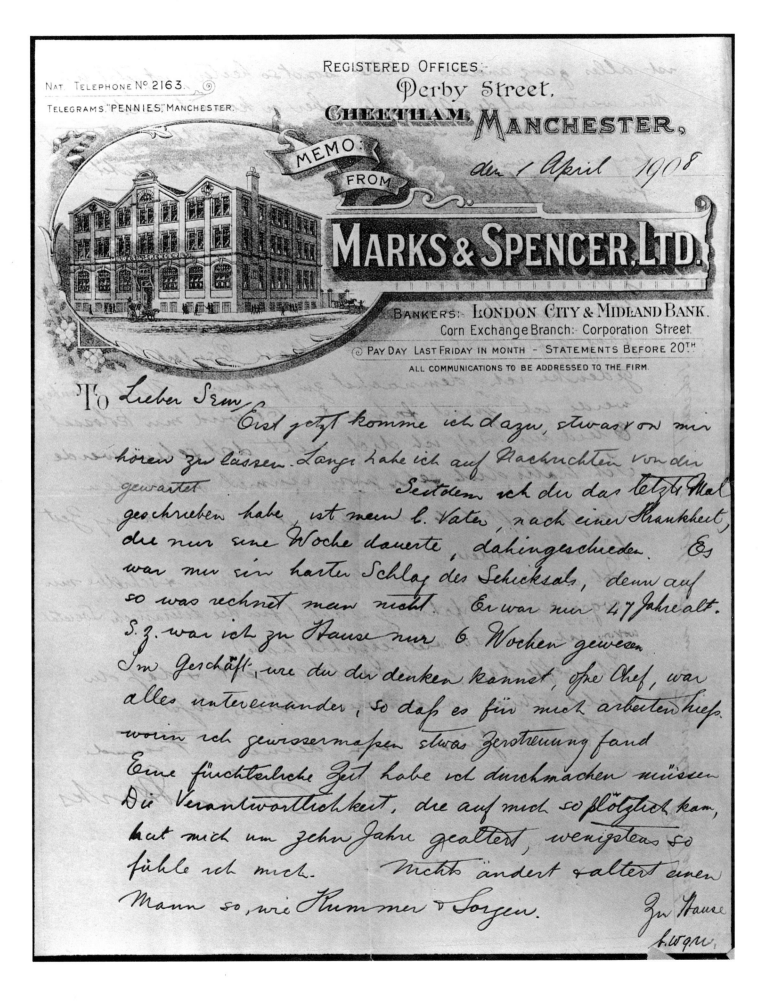

NAT. TELEPHONE Nº 2163.
TELEGRAMS "PENNIES" MANCHESTER.

REGISTERED OFFICES:-
Derby Street,
CHEETHAM, MANCHESTER,

MEMO: FROM

den 1 April 1908

MARKS & SPENCER. LTD.

BANKERS: LONDON CITY & MIDLAND BANK.
Corn Exchange Branch: Corporation Street.
PAY DAY LAST FRIDAY IN MONTH - STATEMENTS BEFORE 20TH
ALL COMMUNICATIONS TO BE ADDRESSED TO THE FIRM.

To Lieber Sem,

Erst jetzt komme ich dazu, etwas von mir hören zu lassen. Lange habe ich auf Nachrichten von dir gewartet. Seitdem ich dir das letzte Mal geschrieben habe, ist mein l. Vater, nach einer Krankheit, die nur eine Woche dauerte, dahingeschieden. Es war mir ein harter Schlag des Schicksals, denn auf so was rechnet man nicht. Er war nur 47 Jahre alt. S.Z. war ich zu Hause nur 6 Wochen gewesen.

Im Geschäft, wie du dir denken kannst, ohne Chef, war alles untereinander, so daß es für mich arbeiten hieß, worin ich gewissermaßen etwas Zerstreuung fand. Eine fürchterliche Zeit habe ich durchmachen müssen. Die Verantwortlichkeit, die auf mich so plötzlich kam, hat mich um zehn Jahre gealtert, wenigstens so fühle ich mich. Nichts ändert & altert einen Mann so, wie Kummer & Sorgen.

Zu Hause
t.wqu.

they now had no presence on the Board of Directors. Simon, still to achieve his majority, was merely an employee of the company his father had founded. Although 'Marks & Spencer' remained over the bazaars' entrances, no member of either family now attended the company directors' meetings. In fact for two weeks there was only one director – William Chapman – until Simon ensured that Chapman was joined by Bernhard Steel as the representative of the Marks family's interests.

Steel, a Manchester jeweller, had been a great friend of Michael Marks; as events would subsequently prove, however, he was not to be a particularly good choice. Steel, together with Alexander Isaacs, another of Michael's friends, had been appointed as executors of his will. Hannah Marks was the third executor. Simon was also nominated but could not fill the position until he reached his legal majority, then twenty-one. Simon was now very frustrated. From being the personal assistant and heir to the throne of his father, he was demoted now to virtually a hired hand. He resolved that the business would one day again be directed by a member of the Marks family – preferably himself.

With incredible enthusiasm he devoted himself to the service of the company. He soon returned to Europe on buying expeditions to France and Germany, while in Britain he became responsible for a large proportion of the company's buying and prospecting of sites for new stores. Gradually his life returned to a certain normality. His friend Israel Sieff, who was by now courting his sister Becky, visited the Marks's home nearly every day. Israel was an excellent companion and confidant. He was also available to share with Simon the good life of Manchester – and good life there was in plenty.

Edwardian Manchester had much to offer wealthy young men in the way of enter-tainment. Among the city's cultural facilities – which were second only to London's – was the world famous Hallé Orchestra. The Palace Theatre of Varieties was Manchester's pre-eminent music hall. Among the famous artists who performed there were Vesta Tilley, Charlie Chaplin and Harry Houdini. The classics were offered at the Queens Theatre, where under the management of Richard Flanagan, a great Shakespearean enthusiast, sumptuous performances of the Bard's plays were presented. The Manchester Hippodrome specialized in 'Spectaculars', including animal acts. Manchester was well served with hotels and restaurants for after-show dining, the most prestigious being the massive Midland Hotel (where both Simon and Israel would later celebrate their weddings). As well as 600 bedrooms it featured a roof garden and – a novelty in the early Edwardian period – electric lighting and telegraph facilities.

Simon and Israel's close relationship continued to strengthen and develop. 'We did everything together,' Israel recorded in his memoirs, 'and the sharing made every experi-ence richer, every discovery more exciting, every moment sweeter. We never seemed to disagree, we certainly never quarrelled.' Simon's character was, however, beginning to mature and harden under the pressure of both maintaining his family and making his way in Marks & Spencer. As Israel commented, Simon 'was quick, outspoken, frequently explosive . . . [He] was not naturally affectionate, forbearing, tolerant and full of the milk of human kindness; he had it in him to be aggressive, ambitious and even ruthless.' In future years the ever loyal Israel would often have to placate the victims of Simon's wrath; as he commented, 'I was of a milder temperament, slower to react, more tolerant of the untoward, living at a lower temperature; so much so, that frequently Simon would persuade me to deal with his offenders; he knew I would be more diplomatic.'

Simon and Israel, as they both acknowledged, were fortunate in spending their early lives in Manchester. Founded by the Romans, the town was by the sixteenth century a

Bernhard Steel, executor of Michael Marks's will and a director of Marks & Spencer, appointed in 1908 to represent the Marks family's interests.

Simon Marks (left) and Israel Sieff in their twenties. The pair met at Manchester Grammar School in 1901 and each later married the other's sister.

flourishing wool centre. By the beginning of the eighteenth century it had developed into a market town of 10,000 people; and by 1851 it was a commercial and manufacturing city with nearly one-third of a million inhabitants.

By the 1850s communications had been boosted by the completion of the railway system, followed in 1894 by the Manchester Ship Canal, which allowed ocean-going ships to link Manchester to the world's trade routes via the Mersey estuary and the Irish Sea. At the time of Michael Marks's death, the population of metropolitan Manchester had risen to over $2\frac{1}{4}$ million people. Apart from its theatres and orchestras, Manchester could boast of Britain's leading provincial newspaper, the *Manchester Guardian*, known internationally as a voice of liberalism. The university, located to the south of the city centre, had also acquired sufficient status to attract scientists of the calibre of atomic physicist Ernest Rutherford, the chemist William Perkin, and the philosopher Samuel Alexander.

One of the city's greatest assets was the naturally warm but practical character of the native Mancunians and, as far as Simon Marks and his fellow Jews were concerned, their general acceptance of the 35,000-strong Jewish community in their midst. The community had been founded in 1788 (although Jewish pedlars had visited the city without settling for at least fifty years previously). In that year, twenty German Jews rented small shops in Manchester's run-down Old Town district and within a few years had established those twin tokens of Jewish settlement, a synagogue and a cemetery. By the end of the eighteenth century the original twenty had been joined by German and Dutch Jewish merchants attracted by the possibility of exporting Manchester textiles to the Continent. Among these was the young Nathan Mayer Rothschild, who from 1799 until he moved to London in 1811 dealt in the export of textiles from Manchester to Frankfurt.

Manchester's industrial success instigated further Jewish immigration. At the lower end of the social scale were the penniless East Europeans, who by 1858 made up about one-third of the community, living in the decrepit Red Bank area north of the city centre, where Michael Marks settled in 1894. They were involved, as they had been in the little towns of Russian Poland, in small scale peddling and the manufacture of clothing. At the other end of the social scale were the anglicized Jews, prominent as cotton traders and professional men. Between these extremes, as noted by Manchester historian Bill Williams, was a solid body of modestly successful shopkeepers, still dealing in such traditional Jewish lines as clothing, jewellery and stationery. There was also a small number of Sephardic Jews who set up in business as exporters.

Michael Marks's social ascent has been described earlier. In the process of building up a successful business he had ensured that his good fortune was shared by both needy Jews and non-Jews alike. Within the Jewish community he gave generously to many organizations, including the Working Men's Club and the Soup Kitchen for the Jewish Poor. But even *his* generosity would have been unable to cope with the financial requirements of a community that was now the second largest in Britain after London. Among the facilities established to cater for its requirements were 39 synagogues, 38 charities and social aid societies, 12 educational establishments, 25 friendly and benefit lodges and 8 trade unions.

Simon was certainly not religiously observant. He ate non-kosher food, rarely attended the synagogue and apart from the occasional word in Yiddish spoke English with a soft, north country accent. His friend Israel was similarly non-Orthodox, but had taken his interest in Judaism further at the age of seventeen by joining the World Zionist Organisation.

The event which had provoked this interest had been sudden and dramatic. One day, while standing in the front room of his home in Bury New Road, he heard a commotion in the street outside. He went to investigate and saw a jeering and shouting group of youths chasing two Jewish lads down the street. Although the episode was over in a moment, the boys and their pursuers gone, Israel later related in his memoirs that he was upset and disturbed by the incident. His father, at the back of the house and unaware of the fracas, listened to Israel's account and assured him that 'When the Jews have a country of their own to go to they shall have nothing to fear.'

Until that time, Israel had regarded the Zionist interests of his father as 'somewhat academic, rather above my head, outside the limits of my personal life'. The scuffle outside his home completely changed his outlook. If such an incident, he considered, could occur in democratic and free England, what future could there be for the beleaguered Jewish masses still penned and persecuted within the borders of Imperial Russia? Of the remainder what hope indeed could there be when the ruler of Russia, Tsar Nicholas II, could proudly wear on his uniform the badge of the Union of the Russian People, the so-called Black Hundreds, Russia's most militantly anti-Semitic organization. Similarly, in adjacent Romania, the quarter of a million Jews were being hounded and persecuted by a viciously anti-Semitic regime. In Israel's eyes there was surely only one solution to the 'Jewish problem', and that would be the resettlement of Jews in the land they had been driven from nearly 2,000 years earlier – *Eretz Yisrael*, the 'Land of Israel'.

Israel Sieff's newly found cause inspired his friend Simon, and together they discussed and investigated the movement. Soon they were deeply involved. As much of Simon Marks's life outside Marks & Spencer would subsequently centre on his Zionist activities, it seems appropriate at this point to give a brief historical account of the movement.

The idea of 'the ingathering of the exiles' was not new. For eighteen centuries the Jews had mourned their departure from the Promised Land. The end of the Jewish people as a nation dates from the destruction of Jerusalem and the second Temple by the Romans in the year AD 70. But through their religion the Jews held together. The anniversary of the expulsion is still marked in synagogues with mourning and fasting. To many democratized Jews, however, the longing of a return to Zion was merely a romantic notion. They had no real thoughts of leaving the relative comforts and freedom of the USA and Western Europe for the deserts and malarial swamps of Palestine.

When Simon first became aware of Zionism, Palestine had for 400 years been a province of the Ottoman Turks, who had let it lapse into a state of poverty and decay. A small number of Jews had continued to live there following the destruction of the Temple, joined by others who settled mainly for religious reasons. During the late nineteenth century a few East European Jews had arrived and established small settlements. But there was as yet no intention to re-establish a sovereign Jewish state, simply to settle in the Holy Land.

The modern concept of a Jewish state was the brainchild of Theodor Herzl, a young Austrian writer born in Hungary. In 1894 Herzl represented his Viennese newspaper at the trial in Paris of Captain Alfred Dreyfus, a French Jewish army officer falsely accused of betraying military secrets to foreign agents. Dreyfus was convicted and sent to Devil's Island. The case, and the subsequent retrials before his innocence was proved, became a great cause célèbre at a time when France was influenced by virulent anti-Semitic agitation.

Herzl, a totally assimilated Jew, suddenly became aware just how perilous the Jewish position was, when even in the land of liberty, equality and fraternity, religious bigotry was still endemic. He reasoned that only in a state of their own could the Jewish people find security. In 1896 he published a slim volume expounding his views entitled *Der Judenstaat* (The Jewish State). The book was received with considerable reserve in the West, where assimilated Jews considered that such views would lay them open to charges of dual allegiance by their Gentile neighbours.

Herzl persevered. He sought an audience with the sultan of Turkey and the German kaiser in an effort to draw up a charter that would guarantee a Jewish homeland. So eager was Herzl to achieve a settlement that he was even willing to accept a grant of land outside

Theodor Herzl, the Austrian Jewish writer, who in 1896 published a book (*Der Judenstaat*) which promoted the concept of a return to Palestine as a homeland for Jews.

Palestine in East Africa. This concept was decisively defeated at the World Zionist Conference he organized in Basle, Switzerland, in 1903, when Herzl was astonished to find that among his most obdurate opponents were representatives of Russia's Jews, the very people he thought would benefit most from such a refuge. The message was clear; a homeland outside Palestine, even as a temporary refuge, was out of the question.

Herzl would die a disappointed man the following year at the age of forty-four, worn out and convinced that his mission had failed. He would never know that his pioneering work had established the basis of a movement which within half a century of his death would result in the return to Zion he had so desired.

In the summer of 1903, twenty-two-year-old Oxford undergraduate Harry Sacher was spending his long vacation on a cycling holiday centred on the little German town of Murrhardt in the province of Baden. One day, he received a letter from home informing him that a Zionist meeting was shortly to take place in Basle, and suggesting that he might be interested in attending. Having time on his hands, Sacher set off on his bicycle on the 185-mile journey to the Swiss border town. He arrived on the day before the conference was due to begin and managed to gain entrance to the congress hall by discreetly infiltrating the English delegation. The conference proceedings – which included Herzl's defeat on his proposal for a Jewish homeland outside Palestine – enthralled Sacher, but as a newcomer he was ignorant of many of the matters discussed. Nevertheless he was fascinated by the principles involved, and his lifelong dedication to Zionism was ensured.

Harry Sacher, as yet unknown to Simon Marks and Israel Sieff, would within a few years join them as another brother-in-law, forging the third link in a partnership that would provide not only major financial support but much of the political direction of the Zionist movement. Born in 1881 in London's East End, the son of immigrant Jewish parents, Sacher had progressed from the Jews Free School in Whitechapel, to study at no less than four universities – London, Oxford, Berlin and Paris – acquiring en route a Master of Arts degree.

By 1905 Sacher was living in Manchester and about to start a journalistic career with the *Manchester Guardian*. The newspaper's manager had recruited him during his first year at Oxford University and had subsequently introduced him to the paper's famous editor, C. P. Scott. Scott had been favourably impressed by the young undergraduate, and agreed to Sacher joining his newspaper after 'finishing' in Berlin and Paris.

The year Sacher began work, Simon and Israel were still teenage boys living in Manchester, about to leave school. It would not be for a further eight years, in 1913, that the three young men would join forces under the leadership of a remarkable man, Chaim Weizmann (leading Zionist and first President of Israel, 1949–52), and make Manchester, in the words of Harry Sacher, into 'the fulcrum which moved the Jewish world.'

Weizmann was thirty years of age when he arrived in Manchester in 1904, a few months before Harry Sacher took up his post with the *Manchester Guardian*. The two men may have met at the Basle conference in 1903, where Weizmann had vehemently opposed the notion of a settlement outside Palestine. If not, Sacher would certainly have seen him on the speakers' platform. Weizmann was an impressive, charismatic figure, as is borne out by Israel Sieff's description of their first meeting: '... I was struck by his personality, almost before I had taken in the details of his appearance. It was magical, overwhelming, irrevocable.' Later he wrote, '... the moment I met him he became my master.'

Simon was equally transfixed. In a revealing interview with the Israeli newspaper

Chaim Weizmann, architect of the Zionist movement and later first President of Israel. A research chemist who came to England in 1904 to work at Manchester University, Dr Weizmann became a close friend of Simon Marks and Israel Sieff and inspired their own passionate involvement in Zionism. He also taught them the advantages of the commercial application of scientific discoveries.

Ma'ariv in 1962, ten years after Weizmann's death and fifty years after their first meeting, Simon with passion declared, '... I thank God for the day I met Chaim Weizmann and for the possibility I had to work with him and to bask in the rays of his personality for a few decades.' The journalist went on to ask him how and why the Manchester group had formed. Simon replied, '... I really could not tell you why. Our Lord has his own ways. One thing I know; we in Manchester had the privilege to know and understand the man at the beginning of his road and I shall treasure this privilege for ever and ever.' And treasure it he did – as the journalist observed:

> 'With Simon, Weizmann seems to be still alive. He speaks of him as if he had seen him an hour earlier ... as if he was going to lunch with him at the Dorchester ... for Simon the first President remained in flesh and blood, alive, walking about, doing things, giving advice. It sometimes seems that Weizmann was the best friend Lord Marks ever had.'

Or perhaps a second father. On Weizmann's faults, his dislike of criticism, the occasional biting sarcasm, his lack of organization and contempt for routine, Simon was silent.

Weizmann's Zionism sprang from his experiences in early life. Born in 1874 in Motel, a village in the Pale of Settlement not far from Michael Marks's birthplace in Slonim, Weizmann would describe his home village as one of hundreds where Jews lived, 'as they had lived for many generations, scattered islands in a Gentile ocean'. Initially educated in the village school, Weizmann had moved on to the technical college in the neighbouring town of Pinsk to study chemistry. His passion for the subject and his Zionism grew in parallel during his years at the universities of Freiburg, Geneva and Berlin. While at Freiburg, where he was appointed a PhD, magna cum laude, in chemistry, he was also visiting Russia and illegally espousing the Zionist cause, once narrowly escaping arrest. In 1903 he visited London for the first time, establishing new contacts and investigating the Zionist scene in this – to him – new land. Well before his visit, Weizmann had developed an affinity for Britain and the British. Indeed at the age of eleven he had written in remarkably mature terms a letter to his teacher in the village school at Motel: 'Why should we look to the Kings of Europe for compassion? That they should take pity on us and give us a resting place? In vain! All have decided the Jews must die, but England will nevertheless have mercy upon us!'

There was in Britain, in certain upper-class Gentile circles, a sympathy for the Zionist cause, based on the biblical tradition of the return of the Jews to Palestine. The pressure of Weizmann's activities on the Continent was beginning to overwhelm him. Many of his plans and schemes had foundered and as he later wrote, '... I was in danger of being eaten up by Zionism with no benefit either to my scientific career or Zionism.' It was time for a change, a regrouping. Why not England, Weizmann considered, and why not Manchester, from whose university he had recently received an offer of employment? The city would at least offer him a refuge for a while from mainstream political life on the Continent. He was also aware that when he wished to re-enter the Zionist arena, Manchester's 35,000-strong Jewish community would provide a sound basis for his future endeavours. Of particular importance to Weizmann was the city's position as a major centre of the chemical industry, together with the international reputation of Manchester University's chemistry department.

On 10 July 1904, Weizmann, with eighteen shillings in his pocket and a letter of introduction to William Henry Perkin, Manchester's renowned professor of chemistry, landed at Newhaven. His first position was as an unpaid assistant to Professor Perkin. The

Harry Sacher, a journalist on the *Manchester Guardian* and a leading Zionist and supporter of Chaim Weizmann. He married Simon's sister Miriam and was a director of Marks & Spencer for thirty years.

£6 per annum that he had to pay for the use of his laboratory made considerable inroads into his finances, although the commissions on chemical patents he had registered in Europe helped a bit.

Despite his original intention of avoiding political work, Weizmann was within a few months addressing the Manchester Zionist Association at the invitation of its president, Charles Dreyfus (no relation to Alfred), a Jewish emigré from Alsace. Dreyfus, a member of the East Manchester Conservation Association and a local figure of some distinction, was also owner of the Clayton Aniline Company, a local dye works where Weizmann would shortly be engaged in private research.

Under Dreyfus's patronage, Weizmann had the opportunity to meet the elite of Manchester society, both Jews and Gentiles. He was not impressed, however, by the majority of assimilated English Jews he met. They were, in his eyes, too materialistic, and they had become complacent, perhaps from living in a country where there was little anti-Semitism to fire their Zionist souls. Their Zionism was not his. In the opinion of many English Jews, Zionism was of more interest to their distant and poor brethren in Russia than to them. Weizmann's attitude may at that time have owed something to his difficulties with the English language. However, a year's intense study soon added English – spoken to the end of his days with a thick Russian accent – to the Yiddish, Russian, German, French and Italian languages already in his repertoire.

In 1905 Weizmann met Harry Sacher at a Zionist meeting hosted by Charles Dreyfus. Their views coincided and a lifelong friendship and political association was thereby established. Harry Sacher and Israel Sieff's later marriages to Simon's sisters, Miriam and Becky, would with Simon's marriage to Israel's sister Miriam, form the nucleus of 'The Family' (as they were termed in Zionist circles), a clan without whose passionate involvement in Zionism, the dream of a Jewish homeland might never have been realized.

Israel Sieff's marriage to Rebecca Marks in 1910 was the first wedding among the younger generations of 'The Family' born in England. The ceremony took place on the flat roof of the Midland Hotel, Manchester, under a wedding canopy brought specially from the couple's synagogue in the northern suburbs of Manchester. The bride was twenty and the groom twenty-one. A photograph of the wedding party, with the ladies in bonnets and dressed in Edwardian finery, their menfolk in morning dress, includes many of the people who featured in Simon's early life.

The twenty-two-year-old Simon, as best man, is standing behind his sister Rebecca. His confident stance and smile belie the problems he was facing over the control of Marks & Spencer. (Indeed, a significant absentee from the wedding party was William Chapman, then Chairman of Marks & Spencer.) On Simon's left stands the burly, bearded figure of Ephraim Marks, Michael's brother, who had joined Michael in England having first served as a conscript in the tsar's army in Russia. Ephraim would subsequently open a small chain of Penny Bazaars on his own account, with his brother's financial and practical assistance. They did not prove very successful, however, and the majority closed or were eventually bought out by Simon in the 1920s. To the left of Simon's sister sits their mother Hannah, a rather sad figure, still mourning the husband who had died three years earlier. The mustachioed figure of Bernhard Steel, the representative of the Marks

ABOVE A studio portrait of the newly-wed Israel and Rebecca Sieff. They were married in 1910.
OPPOSITE The wedding party were photographed on the roof of the Midland Hotel, Manchester, after the ceremony.

family on the company's board, stands second right of Simon. He would soon be forced to retire following the financial improprieties of his family's building firm in their dealings with Marks & Spencer.

The Spencer family are also represented on the photograph. Tom Spencer Junior, in the centre of the back line, was, like Simon, employed as a manager in Marks & Spencer. His stepmother, Agnes Spencer, is to his front right. Already in her fiftieth year when the photograph was taken, she would live a half century more, eventually dying in her ninety-ninth year in 1959. Agnes had known Simon almost from his birth and would develop a great regard for him. It was rumoured that Simon's later dislike of bead-type buttons on Marks & Spencer's ladieswear ranges was due in part to Mrs Spencer's habit, when he was a baby, of pressing him to the button-covered bodice of her high-necked dress.

Second in from the left of the row in which Simon stands is Miriam Sieff, the second of Israel's sisters, wearing a white summer dress and broad-brimmed hat. In 1910, the date of the photograph, Miriam was a sixteen-year-old schoolgirl and Simon, six years her senior, was a well-travelled and rapidly maturing businessman. Over the coming years their friendship would develop into a more serious relationship, and eventually marriage.

In the two years prior to the wedding, the clash of personality between Simon and Rebecca had somewhat receded; Rebecca's attentions had been diverted elsewhere. In 1908 she left the Manchester High School for Girls and went to the University of Manchester's women's department to study English. Israel, her fiancé, had enrolled two years earlier to study Economics. So forceful was Rebecca's personality that she convinced

Israel to attend *her* lectures as well as his own. This, she informed her future husband, would prevent his developing a one-track mind!

Marriage was not a priority for Simon at the time of his sister's wedding. Of greater importance was the situation in Marks & Spencer. In 1911 the company had a turnover of £268,000 from eighty-nine shops and stalls. This compared favourably with the turnover of £169,000 from forty-nine units in 1907, the year of Michael Marks's death. There is no doubt that the two directors at this time, William Chapman and Bernhard Steel, were capable businessmen.

William Chapman, the Senior Director, was responsible for accelerating the company's move from market halls and arcades to high street sites, thus facilitating the possibility of future major extensions. If Chapman had at this time resigned the chairmanship of his own original handkerchief business and devoted his total energies to the direction of Marks & Spencer, the future story of the company might have been very different. He

Taken in 1910, this photograph shows an orderly queue of people dressed in their finery moving down Regent Road, Salford, possibly for a celebration of the accession of King George V. In the background is the Marks & Spencer Penny Bazaar, which traded from 1902 to 1932.

might then have prevented Simon from gaining future control of the business. And Simon might have considered joining Israel Sieff in the Sieffs' prosperous textile business, Sieff and Beaumont. Marks & Spencer under Chapman's control might have continued to prosper. It is more likely, though, that without Simon's later dynamic, entrepreneurial skills, the company would have succumbed to a takeover by a rival retailing firm such as the giant American F. W. Woolworth organization, which had opened its first branch in Britain in Liverpool in 1909.

Prior to setting up in business in Britain, the Chairman Mr Woolworth had travelled from his headquarters in America to survey the retailing scene here. He found, according to his biographer John K. Winckler, that the British public were served by so-called 'Penny Bazaars', most of which were in his opinion simply sidewalk stalls offering a very limited variety of goods, generally displayed in baskets. Woolworth concluded that he could crush such opposition with a chain of bright, commodious and well-stocked stores modelled upon his own American establishments. He decided to call his British outlets 'threepence and sixpence' stores, the equivalent of his 'five and dime' stores in the USA. This American critique of Marks & Spencer's retail policy was, of course, unknown to William Chapman and Bernhard Steel, though had they known of it they would not have been particularly worried; Marks & Spencer's sale of penny-only goods was progressing well, apparently little affected by the more expensive American competition.

Unfortunately, despite their successful business partnership, personal antagonism separated the two men, mainly due to disputes on costs between Marks & Spencer and the

The staff of the East Ham branch of the London Penny Bazaar Company in front of the shop, 1911. Three years later the company was acquired by Marks & Spencer.

Steel family's construction business, who were the retailer's building contractors. Their personal differences apart, however, the pair were sufficiently astute to realize that they were managing a most successful and growing business. Each of them had been given 500 shares by the family trusts they represented on their appointment to the board. It was obviously in their mutual interests to increase their shareholding. In July 1909 they proposed an increase of the company share capital to £100,000, in order, they stated, to have extra capital available for the development of the company. Neither the Marks nor the Spencer families had the funds available to take up the offer – a fact known to both men.

Simon was well aware that if Chapman and Steel managed to raise the money either from their own sources or from business friends they would gain control of the company. He accordingly opposed the motion, as did the two family trusts. Some pencilled notes in his handwriting addressed to Chapman objected to the issue of the new shares: '... I trust that after considering the views expressed by me you will see your way clear to act in accordance with such views, particularly having regard to the fact that my family and self are the persons whose interest are at stake.' The proposal was defeated; Simon could again hope eventually to control Marks & Spencer. In January 1911, at the Annual General Meeting, Chapman and Steel again proposed to increase the share capital, this time to £66,000. Surprisingly, the proposal was approved, though never implemented perhaps due to the deterioration of relations between Chapman and Steel.

The board minutes of the period contain numerous references to the acrimonious dispute between the two directors. On 21 August 1912, for example: '... Mr B Steel had shown great laxity and gross carelessness in his arrangement with and supervision of Messrs M & H Steel's work and accounts and their transactions with this firm must cease forthwith.' Even Simon is reprimanded in the minutes for becoming involved in the fracas by approving payments to the Steels which had not been approved by Chapman.

The previous winter, on 28 December 1911, after months of dispute, Simon Marks and Thomas Spencer Junior had been appointed to the Marks & Spencer board. As directors their emoluments were recorded as £300 per annum plus 4 per cent of the profits shared between the four directors. Simon's specific responsibility was minuted as the buying of merchandise, a responsibility he shared with Tom. Simon's board appointment embroiled him further in the Steel affair. On 22 October 1912 the minutes note that '... owing to the unexplained absence of Mr S Marks from business on Tuesday 22nd October 1912 the Directors' meeting was not held owing to being unable to form a quorum.'

No satisfactory explanation of Simon's absence was subsequently recorded in the minutes. The cancellation of the directors' meeting caused by his absence was perhaps a tactic to relieve the pressure on Bernhard Steel who, forced to retire from the Marks & Spencer board in September 1912, was still being held responsible by Chapman for the business transgressions of his brother's firm. The demand for explanations from Steel – as well as his being summoned to directors' meetings at Marks & Spencer – was recorded in the minutes of the almost weekly board meetings. The trauma of all this may have affected the health of this former family friend and executor of Michael Marks's will, for he died a year later.

Simon may have relieved the pressure on Steel, but he was compromising his own position as a Marks & Spencer director. This moral conflict reached crisis point when Chapman instructed Simon Marks and the company solicitor to investigate a final settlement of the Steel affair. One month later Simon was questioned by Chapman, as recorded in the minutes, on his progress:

> '... the Chairman [William Chapman] asked what had he done in the matter
> and as he [Simon Marks] reported no progress enquired if he had any suggestions
> to make and none forthcoming the following resolutions were passed:- that
> W Chapman and T Spencer are going to conduct this case as Mr S Marks
> declined to make any suggestions.'

The tensions on the board so evident in the minutes did not affect the fortunes of the company. In 1912 a record turnover of £316,700 produced profits of £24,000, figures which are more a tribute to the basic soundness of the company rather than the co-

MARKS & SPENCER'S GRAND ANNUAL. 163

THE NEW WAY OF FURNISHING

is to go to MARKS & SPENCER'S PENNY BAZAAR, where for a comparatively trifling outlay you may purchase all the

HOUSEHOLD NECESSITIES

you require. A Special Department will be found at every branch devoted entirely to articles of general utility for the home.

Astonishing Bargains in

Picture Hooks and Suspenders, Picture Nails and Wire, &c., Picture Moulding Hooks, Stair Eyes, Curtain and Cornice Pole Rings, Cup Hooks and Dresser Hooks, Screw Rings and Screw Eyes, Muslin Rod Brackets, Brass-headed Nails, Fancy and Mantel Board Nails, Window Wedges, Lamp Hooks, Butt Hinges, Gate Hooks and Eyes, Hasps and Staples, Draw Pulls, Egg Whisks, Toasting Forks, Ash Pan Knobs, Rack Pulleys, Wardrobe Hooks, Curtain Hooks, Bedstead Knobs, Drugget Pins, Sleigh Bells, Safety Pins of all kinds, Lace Pins, &c.,&c. Collar Supports.

FINGER PLATES
(as illustrated)
with beautiful design in beaten copperware, and highly polished

These are made in a variety of designs, Antique Silver, Oxy-dised, and Brassed, Copper Bronze and Relieved, and a different set may be fixed to every door in your house :: :: Those out of touch with our Bazaars may order direct from Head Depot.

ONE DOZEN PAIR **2/6** CARRIAGE PAID

6 PAIR 1/4½

MARKS & SPENCER, L^{TD.}
ORIGINATORS OF PENNY BAZAARS
DERBY STREET
MANCHESTER

Astonishing bargains advertised in *Marks & Spencer's Grand Annual*, 1909–10. Simon was editor of this first edition.

operation of the directors. Simon's share of the directors' commission for the year amounted to £819 11s 4d.

With the resignation of Bernhard Steel, ostensibly on health grounds, the board was now out of balance. While Chapman and Spencer represented the Spencer interests, only Simon represented the interests of the Marks family trust. Chapman was well satisfied with the arrangement. His influence over a somewhat malleable Spencer guaranteed his control of the company with a 2:1 majority. Any attempt by the Marks family to appoint a fourth director to restore the balance could easily be forestalled by Chapman. He knew that the appointment of a new director could be blocked by the ruling that a 75 per cent majority of shares was required for the appointment.

As the shareholdings of the two families were virtually in the same 50:50 proportion as when the shares had been first issued in 1903, Simon realized that in order to acquire a majority interest he would have to buy the relatively few marginal shares that had been issued to company employees. The cost was heavy: shares valued at £3 each in 1905 (the year Tom Spencer died), had to be purchased by Simon for £12 each in 1913 – and there were 1,000 of them.

MARKS&SPENCER'S CONQUEST OF ENGLAND

BRANCHES EVERYWHERE

M & S
MEANS
MONEY SAVED

Advertisement in the *Grand Annual*, 1913–14, showing the growing number of Marks & Spencer stores in England.

Clearly Chapman, as Chairman, should have allowed the appointment of a new director to replace Steel as a representative of the Marks family interest. He refused to do so. At the company's AGM in February 1913, therefore, Simon Marks proposed the election to the board of Alexander Isaacs, an executor and trustee of his late father's will. A show of hands by the shareholders indicated an impasse – four voted for the resolution and four against. Chapman cast his deciding vote as Chairman against the resolution and declared it 'not carried'. Simon's mother Hannah then demanded a poll of votes, which with proxies showed 16,782 for the resolution and 16,218 against. The Marks family's apparent victory was nullified when Chapman declared the resolution ' . . . not carried because it had not been passed by the requisite majority, pointing out the election of a new director required to be passed as a special resolution.'

Despite this troublesome period on the board, Simon was all the while developing his role as one of the company's two chief buyers. His responsibilities with those of the other directors had been specified on 22 January 1912: ' . . . Messrs. Spencer and Marks undertook the Buying, and other duties to be allotted when a knowledge of the time at their disposal is arrived at.' Chapman was responsible for finance, deficiencies, general expenditure and, as he added in his own handwriting to the minutes, 'such inspecting as might be convenient'. Steel, a few months prior to his resignation, was allocated the estates department, general property maintenance and prospecting for new shop sites.

Simon was responsible, along with Tom Spencer, for the buying of goods valued at one-third of a million pounds per annum. As the majority of merchandise was sold at a penny apiece, the number of individual items involved was colossal. Simon would soon also shoulder some of Spencer's share of the buying due to the director's drink problem, which had already caused his resignation as company secretary. Therefore, while his fellow board members were supervising the secondary, non-buying activities of the business, Simon was developing the entrepreneurial flair, inherited from his father, to seek out and meet his customers' requirements. He was, through practical experience, gaining the one essential skill required by all successful retailers – the ability to buy merchandise.

Penny Bazaar, Holloway Road, 1912; the penny above both windows can be clearly seen, together with the 'Admission Free' sign to entice customers onto the premises.

In his visits to the bazaars Simon would eagerly question the sales assistants – how was this selling? Do the customers prefer the grey or blue darning wool? Which title sells best in the sheet music – *Songs that will never die* or *Songs for the family circle*? What is selling? Why is it selling? Questions, questions, and more questions. With the pattern of the public's requirements clear in his mind, he could then visit his suppliers and specify his requirements.

The company's penny price point was a significant guide to him during the buying exercise. With but one selling price to consider he knew exactly how much he could afford to pay the manufacturer. If the supplier's cost price would not allow him the profit margin he required, his experience would suggest how, for instance, the packaging or some design feature could be modified to allow the necessary cost reduction. The concept of a single price also taught Simon the importance of a simple approach. A specific selling price concentrated the mind of both manufacturer and retailer on how that price could be achieved. It was a lesson that Simon would remember throughout his life. In the 1920s, long after the penny selling point had disappeared, he introduced a five-shilling maximum ceiling price which lasted until 1939. Again for a period after the Second World War he insisted on a £5 maximum for his clothing ranges.

Simon's passion for simplicity was also apparent in his views on ladies fashions. He would enthuse over simple, well-styled garments cut from fine, plain fabrics; the sight of an overstyled dress in a fussy floral print would drive him into a rage. There was, however, little clothing in the merchandise he was buying in 1914. The ranges had in fact hardly changed from the smallware and hardware items his father had sold at the turn of the

ABOVE A partially shuttered frontage at Bath, 1909. The doorway could be secured, while the windows allowed passers-by to see the displays after hours.

RIGHT Staff outside the Penny Bazaar at 12 Broad Street, Reading, 1912.

century. Over the years there had been attempts to sell goods at prices above the crucial penny price point. Between 1908 and 1910, for example, trial merchandise ranges selling at 4½d, 6d and 10½d were tried, but proved unsuccessful.

This seeming inability by the public to associate M&S with anything but the cheapest end of the market did not seriously concern Simon Marks; the young buying director was content simply to satisfy his customers' existing requirements (the concept of offering the public relatively high priced but also high value merchandise still lay some years in the future). Nevertheless, M&S continued to experiment on ways to increase sales under William Chapman's cautious control.

Simon Marks and Miriam Sieff around the time of their marriage in 1915.

In 1910, the possibility of reducing costs by directly manufacturing a proportion of the merchandise sold by the company was investigated. On behalf of Marks & Spencer Simon bought a small business, the Tower Brush Company, for £150. The Brush Company did not thrive under the new management, and in 1913 was sold back to its original owner for £25. A move into food manufacturing was similarly short-lived, following the purchase of a controlling interest in Simpsons Ltd, manufacturers of lemon curd. Virtually the entire Marks & Spencer Board of Directors appointed themselves Directors of the new company. In 1917, just six years after its original purchase, Simpsons was sold back to its founder Mr Simpson at a loss.

The failure of these ventures established a company principle of not dabbling in areas outside its established sphere of excellence – retailing. As Michael Marks had realized years earlier: 'You either make things or you sell them. Don't try both!' A more positive aspect of this principle was demonstrated with the purchase by the company of several rival penny bazaar organizations. The acquisition of these small chains that had attempted to emulate M&S's success, usually in towns where the company was not represented, proved a sound investment.

In 1914, for example, the purchase from the London Penny Bazaar Company of thirty shops plus a warehouse for £15,000 allowed Marks & Spencer an effective entrée into the lucrative London market. Not only did the purchase price include LPBC's entire stock, but as the two companies' shop frontages were virtually identical, only a simple alteration to the nameplate over the entrance doors was required to indicate the change of ownership. The takeover had been negotiated on a particularly amicable basis, and immediately the purchase was completed a celebration party was organized at London's Trocadero club by LPBC's original owners, the brothers Joseph and Louis Esterman. Simon attended the party, at which the star attraction was a large wedding cake surmounted by a small flag bearing a single word – 'Success!'.

So, on the eve of the First World War, the twenty-six-year-old Simon Marks held an enviable position. He was financially secure and the Director of a successful and prosperous business – albeit in conflict with the Chairman. The growing dividends from the Marks family's shareholding in the company were also providing a satisfactory income for his mother and three unmarried sisters. The oldest sister Rebecca, now married to Israel Sieff, had by 1914 provided the family with a new generation and Simon's first nephews – Michael and Marcus Sieff – who later became directors of the company; Marcus was to follow his uncle Edward as Chairman.

Simon was now engaged to Israel Sieff's sister Miriam, a dark-haired, pleasant-natured, rather retiring young lady, who would show the necessary character to cope with Simon throughout the course of their forty-nine-year marriage. The couple married on 27 July 1915 at the Midland Hotel, Manchester. Among the wedding guests was Chaim Weizmann, who one year earlier had been introduced to Simon by Israel. Weizmann's signature as a witness appears on the wedding certificate.

A copy of Simon and Miriam's marriage certificate, dated 27 July 1915 and witnessed by Chaim Weizmann.

Despite his happy domestic situation and all-enveloping Zionist interests, Simon's priority was still to gain control of Marks & Spencer by taking the place of the Chairman William Chapman. For a while this ambition had to be set aside, however, due to a conflict on a very much greater scale. On 4 August 1914 Britain's War Office dispatched the War Telegram to the nation's armed forces – 'War: Germany: Act.'

CHAPTER FOUR

War – In the Trenches and in the Boardroom

O ne week after the outbreak of war, the company's first wartime directors' meeting was held at the Derby Street registered office on 11 August 1914. Tom Spencer, William Chapman and Simon Marks were present. The board had yet fully to appreciate the impact of the war. They naively questioned, for example, the refusal of the Austrian Bank to deal with Marks & Spencer on a property deal – a not unreasonable stance considering the bank's owners were now officially sworn enemies of the British Crown. The directors did, however, consider as far as was possible the initial impact of the conflict and passed a resolution '. . . that business for the present be carried on as usual, and that the Supervisors be instructed to curtail expenses wherever possible on their respective grounds.'

Simon had his own problems to consider. By 1914 most of his savings had been used up in buying the 1,000 company shares owned by outsiders that controlled the balance of power between the Spencer and Marks shareholdings. 'The price was high and exorbitant,' he later wrote, '£14,000 for 1,000 shares; Israel was insistent that the money be found. My mother gave half her savings £5,000. I possessed about £2,500 – my uncle Ephraim Marks contributed about £1,000 and the rest came from my father-in-law.' In addition, Israel Sieff drained his personal account to help his friend. It was the first time he had withdrawn money in quantity. His bank manager, a family friend, asked whether his father Ephraim knew of the withdrawal: 'No,' replied Israel, '. . . and I don't want him to, he would worry.'

One minor shareholder, perhaps doubting Simon's financial solvency, insisted on receiving payment for his shares only in the form of Bank of England notes. The company accountant Mr Kenyon, also a small shareholder, had sufficient confidence in Simon to receive his reimbursement by personal cheque.

Simon reflected in later years on how the money was obtained: 'It says much for their confidence in me, as then wholly untried, that they were willing to support me in so costly a fashion. It was Israel again whose faith in me has never dimmed over the years who helped me to face the first real financial trial of my life.'

The young man who could inspire such confidence in others was not at first glance a particularly impressive figure. Not very tall – 5 ft $6\frac{1}{2}$ in – and rather portly and fully fleshed about the jowls, he resembled the contemporary American comedian Eddie Cantor. Under neatly parted black hair and heavy eyebrows – a family trait – were piercing, dark brown eyes. While at business he was normally serious and unsmiling in manner, at home however he could relax completely, even to the extent of rendering in a soft baritone voice, selections from his repertoire of music-hall songs.

It was Simon's personality which commanded respect and attention. He was naturally confident, even masterful and arrogant by nature, and these qualities were further sharpened by both the weight of his family responsibilities and his self-imposed mission to achieve control of Marks & Spencer. The soft, measured tones of his voice compelled the

Simon displaying an air of earnestness despite the resemblance to his contemporary, the comedian Eddie Cantor.

Penny Bazaar on a corner site at 9/11 West Green Road, Tottenham. It traded from 1905 to 1936.

full attention of his audience, a characteristic which when combined with an upright stance helped deny his lack of height and gave an impression of aloofness and reserve. The overall effect was of a man of substance, supremely confident in his abilities, able to command attention not by his physical presence, but by his unique force of character.

Simon's impatience, and his uncompromising quest for perfection could inspire fear in his staff and suppliers, and apprehension even in those whom he admired. He could be very cruel in his usually justified criticisms, and often left senior colleagues pale and shaken in his wake. He was aware of this, however, and often sought a later opportunity to apologize. Among the few people in his personal circle that commanded his respect were, of course, Israel Sieff and Chaim Weizmann, whom he would often simply – and significantly – address as 'Chief'.

Above all, Simon had the supreme ability to think clearly and unerringly determine the heart of the matter. He was already beginning to realize that Marks & Spencer was developing into more than a group of shops. The company was providing a public service to millions of working-class people whose average wages in 1914 were well below £2 a week. Few could then afford to spend more than a few pennies on items outside the sheer essentials of life. For such people Marks & Spencer was a godsend. A generation earlier, working-class folk had gathered around his father's market stalls on Friday nights and Saturdays to meet, talk and select from Mr Marks's latest penny ranges. In a similar way the larger high street shops of the 1914 period also became meeting places. By now the stores were situated in high streets around the country, with over a third trading in the London area.

Customers entered the typical M&S shop through a wide, welcoming entrance over which was positioned the 'Admission Free' sign, just beneath the fascia bearing the company's name which was illuminated in the evenings by gaslight. The entrance continued as a gangway to the rear of the shop. On either side and around the far end was a continuous horseshoe-shaped wooden counter behind which sales staff tended the merchandise and gathered in the public's pennies. The range of items available for a single penny coin was incredibly large and included haberdashery, fancy goods, stationery, confectionery, tools, tinware, household items, toys and chinaware.

Stock was delivered to the bazaars from the company's warehouses, the largest located within the business's head office in Derby Street, Manchester. Stock in the bazaars not immediately required for display was conveniently stored in rooms above the sales floor, which was at street level. Shops were secured at night by roller shutters. To allow free access during trading hours the frontage was open to the elements – convenient for the public, but unbearable for the sales staff in bad weather. Later, the installation of plate-glass windows and a simple heating system went some way towards relieving their discomfort.

A manageress supervised the staff, up to ten in number in the larger units, and was also responsible for the banking of the day's takings and general administration. The staff worked long hours for pay which, while low, was relatively generous in comparison with other retailers. A newly recruited fourteen-year-old sales assistant would earn five shillings a week, while her manageress earned 25 shillings. For this sum the staff would be expected to work for a minimum of sixty-three hours per week, which was reduced to fifty-three hours with the passing of the Shops Act in 1912.

Despite the harsh working conditions, there was a happy unity among the shop staff and a pleasant reception for that 'nice Mr Marks' whenever he visited on a 'probing' mission. For Simon, the sales assistants were the most important people on the company's payroll; they could do no wrong. His criticisms were always reserved for management. In his view only the sales assistant, who was in direct contact with the customer, could reveal the true reasons why an item did or did not sell. Sales reports and statistics afforded information in bulk, but could not, he felt, dig below the surface and reveal the essential truth surrounding an item of merchandise. Neither could they indicate lost potential sales.

Simon maintained this conviction throughout his business career. In later years he would often dismiss the store manager with a wave of his hand, and with a sales assistant or floor supervisor in attendance would examine and discuss the skirt lengths of a ladies dress or the uneven stitching on the collar of a man's shirt. Sales staff who knew the details of their merchandise became his favourites, and the manager of a store regularly visited by Simon Marks would have to provide a very good reason for transferring Miss Jones, the expert on men's shirts, to say, ladies blouses.

Meanwhile, in the boardroom, the early stages of the war had not brought the two factions on the board any closer. The clash of personalities between William Chapman and Simon Marks was inevitable. Both men were tough, uncompromising characters, well-matched for the final struggle for control of Marks & Spencer. By their very nature

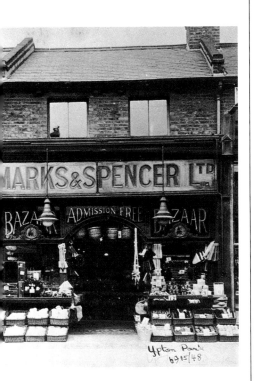

The Bazaar in Green Street, Upton Park, in London's East End, which opened in 1914. The goods are neatly displayed in baskets on the pavement.

they had to lead in any organization in which they were involved – no Board of Directors could have long survived their rivalry. Chapman's advantage as Chairman was diminished by his need to devote a large amount of time and effort to his handkerchief manufacturing business. Simon, in contrast, though able to devote his business hours entirely to the company, had become very involved in his role as personal assistant to Chaim Weizmann.

Weizmann, now a naturalized Briton and the acknowledged leader of British Zionism, was busy promoting the concept of a Jewish homeland in Palestine among the leaders of Britain's press and government. Among the latter were C. P. Scott, editor of the influential *Manchester Guardian*, and Herbert Sidebotham, a senior correspondent on the same newspaper. Scott had in turn arranged a meeting with Weizmann and his own personal friend, David Lloyd George, then Chancellor of the Exchequer in Asquith's wartime cabinet. Lloyd George, as Israel Sieff wrote in his memoirs, '... took a great fancy to Weizmann. It was partly the instinctive appreciation of one great man for another, partly the Welshman's love and understanding of the Old Testament story fortified by an imperialistic sense of what the foundation of a Jewish state on the Suez Canal could do for British interests in that area.' Apart from Lloyd George, Weizmann was also developing his contacts with Arthur Balfour and Winston Churchill. The latter, then a young Member of Parliament, had in 1906 invited Weizmann to speak on his platform when he contested a Manchester constituency which included the Jewish Cheetham Hill district.

Weizmann's income as a lecturer in chemistry at Manchester University was then still insufficient to meet both the costs of his travelling around the country on Zionist lecture tours, and his frequent visits to London to meet the government ministers who were sympathetic to his Zionist views. Simon and Israel Sieff therefore alternately paid for Weizmann's railway tickets and hotel expenses on his journeys to the capital.

To Simon, Weizmann's Zionism satisfied both his love for Britain, the land of his birth, and his natural desire to help find a secure home for his fellow Jews who lived in less pleasant lands. But his hopes were by no means shared by all Britain's Jews. The assimilated aristocratic Jews whose families had lived in Britain for generations were usually vehemently anti-Zionist. They regarded themselves as Englishmen of the Jewish faith. They neither wanted nor needed a home outside the United Kingdom. As Edwin Montagu, a member of such a family and a senior parliamentarian, wrote to his ministerial colleagues:

> 'I assert that there is not a Jewish Nation. The members of my family, for instance who have been in this country for generations, have not the sort or kind of community of view or of desire with any Jewish family in any other country beyond the fact that they possess to a greater or to a lesser degree the same religion . . . .'

Other groups of Jews who opposed a separate Jewish homeland included the ultra Orthodox, who abhorred the very concept of a Jewish state founded by mere mortals. In their view only the Messiah could lead Israel to freedom and establish an ideal kingdom in Palestine. The majority of Britain's quarter of a million Jews were not convinced either way.

To overcome this inertia, Chaim Weizmann intended to publicize Zionism not only among Britain's Jews but also to carry the message to Britain's political leadership. The war had split the international Zionist movement along the national boundaries of the warring nations. In the trenches, German Jews fought British Jews. To the disgust of many recent immigrants to Britain from Russia, Britain was now allied with the very land that had so recently persecuted them and forced them to emigrate. Amid this turmoil, control of the Zionist movement shifted to Britain. Weizmann seized his opportunity. He saw that Britain's war aims – for a while at least – coincided with Zionist aspirations. In a letter, probably drafted by Simon Marks, to C. P. Scott in November 1914 Weizmann acknowledged that although the Jews were too few to claim anything,

'... we can reasonably say that should Palestine fall within the British sphere of influence, and should Britain encourage a Jewish settlement there, as a British dependency, we could have in twenty to thirty years a million Jews out there, perhaps more; they would develop the country, bring back civilization to it and form a very effective guard for the Suez Canal.'

A London Penny Bazaar Company shop, showing the wide entrance that was open all day to the elements and the dust of the road. The sales assistants served from behind the counters arranged in a horseshoe shape around the sales floor.

The letter affirmed that the Zionist and British war aims were as one. Thus would Simon, as political aide-de-camp to Weizmann, gradually become involved with the people of influence who helped shape government policy.

It is a reflection of Simon's single-mindedness that he was virtually able to separate his activities on behalf of Weizmann from his business problems. And business problems there were aplenty. By 1915 Marks & Spencer was beginning to feel the economic effects of the war. Government restrictions and requisitions together with rising building costs had forced the cancellation of many shop developments. The supply of merchandise imported from allied countries for the existing shops was declining, while the flow of goods from

Germany and Austro-Hungary had completely ceased. As a final tightening of the screw, the cost of British-produced goods was on an ever-increasing upward spiral. The combination of these supply factors forced the end of Marks & Spencer's proudly declared aim to supply the public's basic requirements for a single penny. By 1915 the penny price tickets had disappeared from the bazaar's counters for ever.

The leather-bound Minute Book of the time, inscribed in the fine copperplate hand of Mr F. M. Smith, the Company Secretary, recorded some of the most important events in the early history of Marks & Spencer. Perhaps the most significant consists simply of his listing of the names of the five directors attending a board meeting on Monday 20 December 1915: 'Present: Wm Chapman in the Chair; T. Spencer; S. Marks; I. M. Sieff; A. Isaacs.' Simon Marks had now been joined on the board by his friends Alexander Isaacs and Israel Sieff, thereby ensuring virtually certain control of the company.

The struggle for this position had begun in 1913 when Simon had acquired a controlling number of shares and proxies – 16,782 out of the 33,000 shares issued – in an attempt to secure the election to the board of Alexander Isaacs. The resolution was declared void by Chapman, making Simon even more determined to oust him. Simon feared that Chapman's policy of restricting stock levels and his intention to halt the purchase of new sites would virtually end the company's progress and expansion. Chapman doubtless had the interest of the company's shareholders at heart when he formulated these policies. He was, however, twenty years older than Simon Marks, and his cautious outlook was in complete contrast to his rival's energetic and optimistic personality.

The beginning of the final struggle between the two men took place on Monday, 22 November 1915 in the boardroom of the company's Victorian redbrick headquarters in Derby Street, Manchester. One week earlier Simon had fired the first rounds of the battle by absenting himself from a directors' meeting scheduled for 15 November; owing to the subsequent lack of the necessary quorum, the meeting could not be held. The intention behind this ploy may have been to discomfort Chapman, who had been outraged by Simon's similar action in 1912.

A page from the company Minute Book recording a meeting held on 20 December 1915.

Chapman instructed the Company Secretary to write to him, 'stating the meeting was adjourned until Wednesday 17th at 2.30 p.m.' Just before the re-scheduled meeting was due to begin a telegram was delivered to Chapman at Lombard Street, London, at 11 a.m. It read: 'Regret cannot attend meeting this week. Will make it convenient to suit colleagues next week.' Chapman was still determined to hold a meeting that same week. Simon was therefore advised by mail that the meeting was further adjourned for two days until Friday, 19 November at 2.30 p.m. Again Simon refused to attend. In a letter to the Secretary he simply stated, 'In reply to your letter of November 17th I regret I cannot attend the meeting tomorrow.' The meeting was finally adjourned to 22 November.

If Simon's unexplained and discourteous absences from the meetings were *not* an attempt psychologically to divert Chapman from the battle to come, then his journey to London on 17 November is difficult to explain. There was no apparent connection with Marks & Spencer or he would have informed Chapman. Possibly he was taking legal counsel concerning his forthcoming attempt to elect Sieff and Isaacs to the board.

There are two personal reasons that may have taken Simon to the capital. About this time Israel Sieff was trying to establish the whereabouts of his eighteen-year-old younger brother William, who at the outbreak of war and immediately after his leaving Manchester Grammar School had volunteered for army service. Following his induction he wrote some letters to his family telling how he was enjoying army life. Then there was silence. On visiting Aldershot, the camp where his brother had been posted, Israel discovered that William was being held in solitary confinement in a windowless and airless improvised cell, beneath the stairs of the house in which he was billeted. He had been there for ten days. The reason for this treatment, as Israel later wrote, was that he had been rude to his sergeant. William's confinement caused him to suffer a mental breakdown and he spent the remaining fifty years of his life in various mental institutions. During all those years he never uttered a single word. Simon may therefore have accompanied Israel to the War Office, where his friend was attempting to find out the facts behind his brother's ill-treatment. Israel never discovered the full details of the affair; 'It was a scandalous case,' he wrote, 'the Minister of War finally intervened, wrote letters of regret and offered compensation to my father.'

If Simon indeed accompanied Israel to London, then it is almost certain that the two visited their mentor Chaim Weizmann, who during the autumn of 1915 had moved to the capital. The reason for Weizmann's departure from Manchester University was primarily due to his development of a fermentation process that allowed the mass production of acetone, a vital ingredient in the manufacture of cordite, a military explosive. Weizmann, who was subsequently seconded to supervise the manufacturing process in plants around the country, found himself based in government offices in Whitehall, nearly 200 miles from his home. Under wartime conditions the rail journeys to and from the capital were taxing and exhausting; Weizmann realized he had to move to London.

He first took rooms in Chelsea in the autumn of 1915, a few weeks before Simon's mysterious trip to the capital. The two men would have found much on the Zionist front to discuss; Weizmann's acetone process, so essential to Britain's war effort, was winning him friends in high places — friends that could help him realize the dream of a Jewish homeland.

The Bazaar at 25 West Street, Reading, completely closed with roller shutters.

Whatever the reason for Simon's absences, on 22 November 1915 he did eventually attend the much-postponed meeting at Marks & Spencer's headquarters in Derby Street, Manchester. There were in fact two meetings held that day. The first was a shareholders' meeting held at noon, with Chapman in the Chair. Present were the entire Board of Directors, plus attendant solicitors and all the company shareholders – *all* comfortably seated in the wood-panelled 30 × 20 ft boardroom!

The reason for the meeting was to seek approval of a resolution signed by Simon, Hannah Marks, Alexander Isaacs and Israel Sieff to appoint Isaacs and Sieff as directors. Chapman straight away asserted that such appointments required a three-quarter majority, and as the Spencer trustees were against the proposal it was useless to put it to the meeting. He would, however, allow a vote. On a show of hands, five shareholders voted for, and eight against, the resolution. Alexander Isaacs then demanded a poll of the number of shares rather than the number of shareholders. Again the proposal was apparently defeated – 16,174 shares were for the resolution, with 16,218 against.

Simon had apparently lost by 44 votes. In fact, he held and declared perpetual proxies on a further 608 shares owned by minor shareholders, which Chapman, on the advice of the company solicitor – also Chapman's personal solicitor – refused to recognize. Despite Simon's protests that the same solicitor had two years earlier recognized the proxies as valid, Chapman declared the resolution defeated and closed the meeting.

Five minutes after the Extraordinary Meeting had ended and the shareholders had filed from the boardroom, an official meeting of the three directors took place. Chapman struck first. He insisted that owing to Simon's frequent absences the quorum of directors at official meetings should in future be only two. Simon protested and asked to have placed on record that his absence had been restricted to the previous week. Chapman correctly pointed out that 'the Minute Book records themselves [already] showed when Mr Marks had been absent from meetings.' Chapman now had the moral advantage. With Spencer's backing he followed up with the surprise appointment to the board of William Norris, a long-serving company executive and friend of the Spencer family. With an assured majority – three from a board of five directors – Chapman then offered to accept Israel Sieff as an additional director.

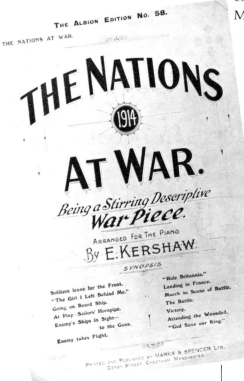

Patriotic sheet music sold during the First World War.

At the same meeting – and despite Simon's objection – Chapman and his acolyte Tom Spencer decided that, 'Considering the internal troubles prevailing . . . all new properties and business matters be dropped for the time being.' This resolution neatly illustrated Chapman's cautious business temperament. By prohibiting discussion and restricting the buying of merchandise (due to his fears of overspending), Chapman intended to force Marks & Spencer into a passive, 'marking-time' position.

Simon was frustrated. He knew that despite wartime restrictions there were still opportunities to exploit in the form of both property and merchandise acquisition. But it was impossible to get his ideas accepted. He realized that the situation in the boardroom could now only be resolved by legal action.

The major technicality to be determined was one of crucial importance. Was Chapman correct in declaring the proxies in favour of Simon Marks invalid? If he *was* correct, then he was also right in declaring the resolution appointing Sieff and Isaacs as not carried and consequently also correct in appointing William Norris as a director. If he was wrong, however, then Isaacs and Sieff by a majority of votes *had* been appointed directors, and with the existing directors – Chapman, Spencer and Marks – totalled five, the maximum number allowed in the Articles of Association. Consequently, William Norris's appointment was invalid, as he would have made an illegal sixth director.

A week later Norris made his one and only appearance at a board meeting as a director. Simon protested at his presence while the matter was subjudice. He also objected to Chapman's refusal, as per his previous resolution, to negotiate on property matters.

Before the next directors' meeting, scheduled for 20 December, the matter had been legally resolved. In the Court of Chancery Mr Justice Peterson ruled that Simon's proxies were perfectly valid and that Sieff and Isaacs *had* been correctly elected directors by the shareholders, thus rendering William Norris's election as a director invalid. Chapman appealed against the decision in January 1916 but the Appeal Court upheld the trial judge's decision; the verdict represented the turning point in the struggle for control of the company.

So, by January 1916 Simon commanded a 3:2 majority on the board; Chapman, nevertheless, was still officially the Chairman of Marks & Spencer. The court's decision against him had, however, jolted him from his customary cautious approach, and discussions on property matters were resumed. The atmosphere at subsequent meetings was still sufficiently acrimonious for the Company Secretary, caught in the cross fire, to request protection for any claims against him following his signing of disputed share transfer forms.

William Chapman continued to oppose Simon's buying strategy. He was concerned over the company's need to meet its ever-increasing costs by borrowing from the banks – a novel situation for Marks & Spencer, which had until 1916 been able to finance its financial requirements from profits put to reserve in previous years. The borrowings were not unreasonable (about £75,000 in 1918) for a company of Marks & Spencer's size; Chapman was apparently unable to appreciate that the business stockholdings had to be increased in order to cushion the effect of wartime shortages. At a directors' meeting on 10 April 1916 he therefore secured an agreement from the board that 'In view of the heavy stocks held, it is recommended that the buying be restricted as much as possible.'

By the spring of 1916, apart from Tom Spencer, who frequently absented himself from board meetings and was to die within the year, Simon was the only full-time director on the board. The responsibilities now allocated to him included the majority of the company's buying, supervision of the London and suburban branches, and prospecting for new sites in the southern half of England. He was also responsible for looking after the company's interest in the firm of Marschner, a French company based in Paris, which acted as agents for Marks & Spencer in France.

It was an involvement that called for Simon's attendance in person, and therefore entailed a number of wartime channel crossings by ferry. The presence of the Royal Navy ensured that there was rarely any hostile interference with passenger shipping or the troop ships that carried reinforcements for the British army on the Western Front. The sight of such ships would no doubt have brought home to Simon the possibility of being called up – conscription had been brought in by Parliament in January 1916.

His best friend Israel had already volunteered for a local Lancashire regiment, the Derby Fusiliers, at the beginning of the war and with his friends, as he later wrote, '. . . marched, drilled, drank beer, got thoroughly fit and enjoyed ourselves while our parents at that stage of the war fumed at what must have seemed to them a monstrous waste of time and energy.' Israel's father was particularly annoyed at this. His business was now providing material for the manufacture of military guncotton and he found himself unable both to supervise the processing and to seek out the raw materials. He needed his son's assistance and so, without seeking Israel's permission, applied successfully for his son's military discharge.

Simon's situation was different. Though like Israel married, he was also supporting his widowed mother and two sisters – the epileptic Tilly and the thirteen-year-old Elaine. As well as that he was the virtually irreplaceable buying director of a company that supplied the household requirements of many thousands of British people. He decided against volunteering for the armed forces, a decision with which William Chapman surprisingly agreed. The choice, however, would soon be out of Simon's hands. In January 1916 Parliament passed the Military Service Act, which introduced compulsory military service for all unmarried men between eighteen and forty-one. In May 1916 conscription was extended to married men as well. Simon could therefore soon expect to receive his call-up papers.

While Simon was struggling with hostile colleagues on the board of Marks & Spencer, and considering the problems which would result from his imminent conscription, he was becoming ever more involved with Weizmann and the Zionist cause. At a time when the possibility of an Allied victory in the Great War was in considerable doubt, Weizmann, a naturalized Briton since 1910, was counting on a British victory. Since the beginning of December 1916 and the ousting of Prime Minister Asquith, Weizmann's friends and admirers had occupied high political office in Britain's government – David Lloyd George was now Prime Minister and Arthur Balfour his Foreign Secretary. Both men held exaggerated views of the power of British Zionists to influence their counterparts in America in bringing the United States into the war. Britain's political leaders were also tempted by the possibility of a large and friendly Jewish community in Palestine forming the basis of a new war front, which would relieve the stalemate in Europe. A friendly Jewish presence in Palestine to replace the Turks with whom Britain had been at war since 1914 would also provide a safeguard for the Suez Canal, Britain's maritime link with the Empire in the East.

There were obstacles for Weizmann to overcome before he could establish the basis of a Jewish homeland under British aegis. For instance, plans existed of which he was then unaware for a pact between Britain and France to form a condominium over Palestine which would frustrate his aims for an eventual Jewish state. In addition, certain influential and aristocratic Jews were making their anti-Zionist views apparent both in the columns of *The Times* and in the Cabinet Office.

At this crucial time Weizmann needed able and loyal men about him. As ever, Simon, Israel and Harry Sacher rallied to his assistance. In early 1916 they rented a three-room suite of offices at 175 Piccadilly in the heart of London's West End from the accountant who worked for Ephraim Sieff, Israel's father. The yearly rent of £150 was paid by Simon. The idea, as Israel later explained was '... to have a bureau from which Weizmann could operate, an office for research, correspondence and official meetings with the Foreign Office men.' From these offices, known as the Palestine Bureau, a monthly journal, *Palestine*, was published, to represent the views of the British Palestine Committee (as the small group called itself). 'The object was to publicize the Zionist Cause,' Israel later wrote, '... and to try to impress everybody with the importance and resources of British Zionism. We were a lobby. Simon and I put up the money, Harry Sacher edited the journal, and Herbert Sidebotham wrote most of it with occasional pieces from Harry and myself.'

Palestine affirmed the aims of the group on the front page of each issue: 'The British Palestine Committee seeks to reset the ancient glories of the Jewish nation in the Freedom of a new British Dominion in Palestine.' Simon organized the administration, dealt with Weizmann's vast amount of correspondence during his frequent absences from London, and kept his mentor informed by cable and mail of political events (gleaned from both the press and visitors to the office) which affected the movement. It was an absorbing task, which allowed him to exercise his initiative to the full and play a role at the centre of major events.

Meanwhile Simon, with an assured 3:2 majority at Marks & Spencer board meetings, began a campaign to undermine Chapman's position. For instance, a reallocation of responsibilities by Simon details 'buying for the Company's smallest warehouse to Tom Spencer', a designation to which both Spencer and Chapman strongly objected. In April 1916 Simon dismissed the company solicitor. No reason was given, but the man who was Chapman's personal solicitor had also declared Simon's perpetual proxies invalid, a decision subsequently overthrown by the Court of Chancery. He was professionally vulnerable and an obvious target for Simon's displeasure. Simon would later tidy up the proxy situation in May 1917 by formally acquiring the underlying shares, thus bringing the Marks family holding to above the critical 50 per cent level. Again Chapman and Spencer objected — as they did later that same month when Simon forced through a resolution to increase the directors' emoluments.

Despite the board's lack of harmony, the directors still collaborated in the day-to-day running of the company. Potential sites for new shops were evaluated, existing shops visited, stocktaking results discussed and, where necessary, action taken. Letters were also dispatched to area and shop management giving instructions on operational matters. One such letter dating from this period, unsigned but probably written by Simon, enshrines principles that would not be inappropriate today:

'... the writer has noticed on going round several branches that the prices of certain articles are not shown and as the assistants are not always conversant with the lines that should be sold at $1\frac{1}{2}$d instead of 1d it must often happen that $1\frac{1}{2}$d goods are sold for 1d.

Then again it is necessary that goods should be plainly marked so that customers

Chaim Weizmann in Palestine, 1917. Israel Sieff, also wearing a light-coloured suit, can be seen in the row behind.

can see for themselves without asking, what is the price of the particular article he requires . . . .'

In August 1916 Chapman complained bitterly that buying during the last six months had been most 'extravagant' and that branches had '2, 3 and even 4 times their normal and requisite stocks'. The heavy stock level was, he stated, 'imperilling not only the income on the trust shares, but jeopardizing the security of the capital.' Though Israel Sieff responded by claiming the criticisms were 'unjust and unfair to the Board' and that 'The buying had been done for the whole year and not for the first six months due to the war supply situation', Chapman's proposal to examine outstanding commitments with a view to cancelling them was surprisingly seconded by one of Simon's 'team', Alexander Isaacs.

This apparent peace offering was immediately withdrawn when Isaacs demanded of Tom Spencer whether he had considered the matter of his resignation from the company, a subject broached at the previous meeting. Spencer retorted that he would neither retire nor resign as a director. Isaacs, backed by Israel Sieff, then insisted that a special meeting be called to 'remove Mr Spencer from the Board of Directors for reasons well known to the Board' – in other words, his excessive drinking. Chapman stood by his one ally on the board and would not approve the resolution; his objection would be the last he would officially make as Chairman of Marks & Spencer.

At a tense meeting during the afternoon of 24 August 1916, Alexander Isaacs, jeweller and executor of Michael Marks's will, moved a resolution that 'Mr Simon Marks be elected Chairman of the Board of Directors of Marks & Spencer Ltd. and that he now take the Chair.' Neither Chapman nor Spencer cast their votes. Instead Chapman in a fit of pique declared the meeting closed and stormed from the boardroom with Spencer following close behind. It was a complete victory for the twenty-eight-year-old Simon Marks. As the door closed behind the stooping figure of Tom Spencer, the remaining directors considered the interesting legal point of whether the retiring Chairman had the power to close the meeting. Israel Sieff, perhaps prepared for such an eventuality, pointed out that a chairman did not have the right to 'stop or adjourn a meeting at his own will'. If he did so insist, then the meeting could appoint a new chairman 'to go on with the business for which it had been convened'. Which is precisely what happened.

To Simon, the instant of his appointment as Chairman of Marks and Spencer must have been a moment of supreme satisfaction. Still in his twenties he had, through his own efforts – though backed by a sympathetic family and friends – regained control of the company which his father had founded thirty-two years earlier. Once again the 'Marks' in the Marks & Spencer sign over the entrances to the nationwide chain of 150 shops carried real meaning for him. As Simon recalled over forty years later:

'I had been engaged for many years in fighting for my position in the firm. After succeeding in that fight I was able for the first time to examine the broad strategy of the company, unhampered by unsympathetic and hostile colleagues.

My life had been made wretched for many years by them. I considered the business as the life work of my father and which in the spirit of those days I was called upon to follow up and to build on his foundations.

On looking back I shudder to think of the inadequacy of the board and its general management. Nothing new in ideas or administration had been evolved but more shops were added. It says much for my father's principles of operation that the business could prosper under such conditions.'

Simon's appointment as Chairman did not immediately remove William Chapman from the Board of Directors; he and Tom Spencer still retained their directorships. Also, despite an appeal by Simon for harmonious working among the directors, plus the appointment of a member of the Spencer family to act as peace intermediary with Chapman, the former chairman continued to block essential revisions of the company's Articles of Association.

The situation could not continue. On 14 June 1917 Chapman and Spencer were finally forced to resign. Chapman made an abortive legal attempt at reinstatement to the board and retained a shareholding in Marks & Spencer until its flotation as a public company in 1926. Similarly, Marks & Spencer continued to buy handkerchiefs from Chapman's firm for several years after his resignation.

Chapman had been a hard-working and driving manager who had contributed much to the early development of the company. He had converted the 'back of an envelope' practices of Mr Marks & Mr Spencer into a much more sophisticated form of administration. For the four years prior to his resignation he had been responsible for the general finance and stock accounts of the business; he had also negotiated the leases for all company properties bought and sold during that period. It was perhaps unfortunate for this tough, capable and diligent man that in Simon Marks he was faced with a character of similar determination. Chapman lived for a further twenty-six years following his resignation and died in Manchester in 1942 at the age of seventy-two. At his death his estate was valued for probate purposes at over £124,000.

Tom Spencer Junior had a much sadder end. On 13 July, exactly one month after his resignation from Marks & Spencer and two weeks after his conscription into the army, he died at Woolwich Barracks at the age of thirty-five. His death certificate gave 'delirium tremens' as the cause of his death. Simon attended his funeral in Southport. Tom was buried near the home that the Spencer family rented annually for their summer holidays.

Simon, too, had by now been conscripted, despite an appeal to the tribunal. The basis of his objection was noted in the company records as simply, '. . . it is important in the interest of the Company that Mr Marks be retained.' On 14 May 1917, Simon was posted to Forward Barracks in Preston, Lancashire. Three days after his induction, he wrote a letter to Chaim Weizmann:

Gunner Marks in uniform, July 1917.

> 'My dear Dr Weizmann, I take the first opportunity of writing you since I have
> taken the King's shilling. I have been posted to the Royal Field Artillery and for
> the moment am stationed in Preston. It was not possible to be transferred to units
> other than those vacant at the time of joining. I am sorry not to be with Jabotinsky
> [a Zionist leader], on the other hand I am quite pleased that I was able to be posted
> to the Artillery which seems more interesting than infantry work. So far as the life
> is concerned, it is "abrutrissant" [brutish]. The dull monotonous atmosphere is
> most trying but like Micawber I am waiting for something to turn up which will
> put an end to this universal madness and which will permit people to be just
> ordinary workaday people and allow them to resume their normal life.'

Later in the same letter, while commenting on Zionist affairs, he wrote: 'It is only by constant reiteration and by occasionally differing from the authorities if need be that one drives home one's point of view.'

Simon would put his theory of 'constant reiteration' into practice countless times over the ensuing years. His concepts of quality and value would be dinned into his business colleagues again and again.

A few weeks before Simon's call-up, his mother Hannah, aged only fifty-five, died suddenly at her home in Manchester, where she lived with her daughters Tilly and Elaine. Simon and his wife Miriam were staying at the time with the Weizmanns in London. Weizmann woke Simon with the news in the early hours of Saturday morning, 20 April 1917. Four days earlier Simon had taken leave of his mother prior to his journey to London. 'She was lying in bed,' he later wrote, '... she took me in her arms, kissed me passionately on my eyes, nose, mouth and drew me tightly to her. She was unusually demonstrative. This so surprised me and filled me with such emotion that I wept bitterly. She was saying goodbye.'

As Simon mourned the passing of his mother, events of vital importance were occurring around the world. In Russia, the 400-year-old Romanov dynasty had finally fallen in March 1917 with the abdication of the last Tsar, Nicholas II, following the disastrous casualties suffered by his armies – two million alone in 1915 – on the Eastern Front. Nine months later the Bolsheviks were in power. In April 1917, President Wilson brought the United States into the war under the slogan 'The world must be made safe for democracy.' In Britain, King George V exhorted his subjects to reduce their bread consumption and thereby free the grain ships for the transportation of more munitions of war. In the trenches the battle of Passchendaele was fought in a sea of mud from January to November 1917; British forces gained a four-mile advance at the cost of 324,000 casualties.

Lord Balfour in 1918. Balfour's letter to Lord Rothschild, written in November 1917 as Foreign Secretary, expressed the British Government's approval of the proposed 'establishment in Palestine of a national home for the Jewish People'; it became known as the Balfour Declaration, and was regarded as a milestone on the road to Jewish statehood.

On the Zionist front, Weizmann, now the uncontested president of the English Zionist movement, made a public announcement in May that Britain supported the creation of a Jewish commonwealth in Palestine. On 2 November 1917, his efforts, together with those of his principal lieutenants Simon Marks, Israel Sieff and Harry Sacher – plus many other ardent Zionists – were finally rewarded when the British Government issued to Lord Rothschild – considered the lay leader of British Jewry – a letter signed by Foreign Secretary Arthur Balfour confirming Britain's favouring '... the establishment in Palestine of a National Home for the Jewish people and will use their best endeavours to facilitate the achievement of that object, it being clearly understood that nothing shall be done which may prejudice the civil and religious rights of existing non-Jewish communities in Palestine.'

This letter, later known as the Balfour Declaration, was in a sense, to the Jews, a 'visa to Palestine'. To persecuted Jewish communities around the world it appeared that a wise power (Great Britain) had recognized their plight and taken them under her wing. The declaration contained ambiguities which would, on reflection, satisfy neither the Jews nor the Arabs, but to Simon and his colleagues it was, at the time, a milestone on the road to Jewish statehood.

A month later, on 11 December 1917, Weizmann's gamble on a British victory paid off when British and Allied forces under General Allenby accepted the surrender of Jerusalem from the Turks. Great Britain, who had favoured the establishment of a Jewish homeland, now occupied the capital of the future state. General Clayton, political officer to the military administration in Palestine, confided to Israel Sieff a year later that the Declaration might never have come about without the Zionist propaganda disseminated in *Palestine*, the journal published by Simon Marks and his friend at 175 Piccadilly, London.

Weizmann was now in the unique position of being virtually the head of state of a country which had yet to be founded. He needed trusty and capable lieutenants around him to help maintain the political impetus generated by the Balfour Declaration. Six of his most capable aides were either in Britain's armed forces or liable for military call-up. Three were members of the family – Simon, Israel and Harry Sacher. At the end of May 1917, Weizmann wrote to the director of military intelligence requesting exemption from military service for all six men on the grounds '. . . that as the British military and political enterprises in Palestine ripen, the services of these men may be found to be of the highest value to H.M. Government. Their work is . . . not only of a highly confidential kind but one which calls for exceptional qualifications.' Weizmann continued, '. . . one of them, Mr Marks, joined the army a few days ago and his loss is very severely felt. I would ask that he be restored to civil life and so available for Zionist work . . . .'

Weizmann's request was granted, and 230068 Gunner Marks, who as Chairman of Marks & Spencer had been forced to hold his board meetings in the Bull and Royal hotel and public house, two miles from his barracks in Preston, suddenly found himself returned to civilian life. In later years Simon would recall the transformation in the attitude of his sergeant major when he read the official order releasing him from army service to deal on equal terms with the leading statesmen and military men of the day. As Simon related to Israel, the sergeant major '. . . hastily made it clear to me that the language he had been using when instructing me how to clean the lavatories and shine his boots had been a professional not a personal matter and that he had only been doing his duty. I shook hands with him and said that duty called us all in different ways.'

Between Simon's demobilization and the Armistice on 11 November 1918, the Marks & Spencer board, now free from the constant confrontations between Simon and William Chapman, had settled down to a more regular and placid routine. Two replacements for Chapman and Spencer Junior had been elected to the Board of Directors to represent the interests of the Spencer family – Alfred Davis, a partner in a firm that traded with Marks & Spencer, and John Luther Green, a relative of Agnes Spencer and an assistant town clerk

The Bull & Royal Hotel, two miles from the barracks in Preston, where Simon held his board meetings while still serving in the army.

Note dated 2 July 1917 from Simon returning his uniform to the Quartermaster Sergeant at Preston Barracks; and on the reverse, the receipt.

at Stockton. Only Simon and Alexander Isaacs were full-time directors, the remaining three – Israel Sieff, Davis and Green – served only on a part-time basis.

The board minutes of the period record the beginning of practices that would become standard during Simon's reign as Chairman, and later those of his successors. In July 1918, for example, Simon presented William Norris – who had sided with Chapman in the struggle for control of the company – with a cheque for £200 and a gold watch to

A Zionist meeting in London, 1918, with, on the platform, Simon Marks (front row, far left) and Israel Sieff (second from right); at the table, Chaim Weizmann (left); and Harry Sacher (back row, second from left).

commemorate twenty-five years' service with the company. In 1950 Norris's son, Wilfred, would be appointed to Simon's Board of Directors. Laura MacQuillan, a minor shareholder and the fourth sales assistant and employee in the company who had also sided with Chapman, would decades later in 1959, at the age of seventy-eight, receive a formal presentation from Simon, then Lord Marks. He described her then as 'one of the prettiest girls I ever saw', and 'the oldest link in the business of Marks & Spencer'. In October 1918 the mother of an employee was paid an allowance of £130 per annum while her son was serving in the army. And in April 1918 the company made donations of £105 each to the Zionist Preparation Fund and the YMCA Hut Fund. These early instances of charitable donations, staff welfare and recognition of staff loyalty would be multiplied many times in the coming years.

At the end of the war, Simon decided to move his home to London. The company had, since September 1917, while maintaining the official Head Office in Manchester, rented a London office at Moorgate Hall in the City of London. The capital was now

Simon with his first child, Hannah, born in 1918.

becoming the hub of Simon's business and private activities. Not only was Weizmann living there, but a growing proportion of Marks & Spencer's profits was being generated in the south of England. Simon had also noticed that the number of salesmen who brought their samples to the business's Manchester headquarters had dramatically fallen as the post-war shortage of goods allowed travellers to dispose of their ranges in the much larger and more accessible London market.

By the time of Simon and Miriam's move in 1920 from Didsbury, Manchester, to the leafy heights of Hampstead in north London, the first of their two children, Hannah

Friendly House, Chiswell Street, the London office of Marks & Spencer from 1921. It became the registered Head Office in 1924.

Olive, had arrived. Hannah, born in September 1918, was followed by Michael, born in August 1920. Both children were named after Simon's parents. The Marks's new home in Hampstead, a tall, forbidding house built in Victorian Gothic style and set in half an acre of grounds, was some five miles from the company's London offices, now situated in larger premises at Friendly House, Chiswell Street, in the City of London.

At the time of his move to London Simon was earning £3,500 a year, plus £1,500 expenses and 4 per cent of the company's annual profits above £35,000. He also received considerable benefit from the dividends on his Marks & Spencer shares. His fellow directors voted him an extra £2,500 to cover his removal expenses, stating that in their opinion '. . . Mr Marks will be able to render much more valuable services to the Company from London as his centre and headquarters than Manchester.'

Despite the continuing success of the company – turnover for the 1922 financial year was £677,000, with a profit before tax of £59,000, compared with £29,000 profit in 1921 – Simon was aware of developing problems within the business and in particular of the dangers of competition, specifically from the American-based F. W. Woolworth organization. Marks & Spencer was at this time selling a hotchpotch of merchandise at prices ranging from sixpence to five shillings, while Woolworths had managed to maintain their prices at threepence and sixpence. Simon recalled this competition in a short note written in the late 1950s:

'. . . the size of their stores, the wealth of variety of the goods they offered to the public at up to 6d per article was breathtaking. It was only a question of time when their red signs would dominate the high streets of the country and their name would become justly a household name for value and variety. It soon became obvious that changes in our own approach were essential if we were to survive.'

Simon realized that Marks & Spencer, despite its previous success, had 'no direction, no leadership, no thought'. As for himself: 'That I was apprehensive as to the future, looking back, seems now to be an understatement. I was afraid and the question of how to react, what to do, was my concern, day and night.' Suddenly he saw his shops as they were; down-at-heel emporiums with a clientele who could not dissociate Marks & Spencer from the cheapest end of the retail market. He felt unable to take any pride in either the shops or the goods he sold: the cheap crockery, haberdashery and hardware were too similar to the merchandise his father had sold from his market stall, forty years earlier. Neither did Simon, on a purely personal basis, relish the possibility of being permanently known as the owner of a chain of down-market Penny Bazaars.

The final straw came when a store manager reported to him that some Woolworth directors visiting his store had picked up and examined various articles and had disparagingly referred to them as 'lemons'. Simon was offended but could only agree with their judgement: 'They are right! They *are* lemons!' He came to the conclusion that Woolworths had the cheap end of the variety market tied up in Britain. They were an efficient organization and in their field were able to buy on better terms than Marks & Spencer.

Simon could have attempted to meet the competition by indulging in the uncertainties of a price war. In his office he examined a simple wooden pencil purchased from Woolworths. 'What can I do,' he mused, 'to improve the value of this basic pencil and increase its appeal on the counters of Marks & Spencer?' He realized there was little improvement possible. Neither could he improve the values of similar basic commodities he sold, such as a gallon of paraffin, a rolling pin or a bag of flour. Perhaps, he considered,

Shop frontages varied greatly at this time as these illustrations show. All four stores opened in the space of only two years. RIGHT Church Street, Blackpool, opened in 1923; the second sales floor, with a front wall made almost entirely of glass, was added in 1924.

ABOVE Grange Road, Birkenhead, opened in January 1923.

RIGHT High Street, Cheltenham, opened in November 1923.

he might sell items where value *could* be added by harnessing the benefits of the scientific expertise that his friend Weizmann was forever expounding.

He calmly reviewed his business situation. The company was trading profitably due to the low selling prices of the majority of goods, attracting, during the early 1920s, the growing numbers of unemployed. There were no problems on the business property side, owing to Simon's insistence that wherever possible freehold sites should be acquired rather than settling for the short-term advantages of a lease. He also knew that larger stores were

Castle Street, Bristol, opened in December 1924; the word 'bazaar' has been dropped in favour of 'stores'.

more efficient and better value than smaller units — though a company-wide store design policy had yet to be decided.

The frontage of the older Marks & Spencer units could generally be measured in less than seven paces, and even though new stores opened in the early 1920s had frontages over sixty feet long, with a corresponding depth, the frontage designs varied considerably, indicating perhaps an uncertainty reaching to the highest level of the company's command — to Simon himself. He could hesitate no more. He decided to revive his spirits, reaffirm his ambitions and seek new ideas by setting sail for that land of opportunity and free enterprise — the United States of America.

85

CHAPTER FIVE

Enter Saint Michael

n Wednesday 20 February 1924, the White Star liner *Olympic* slipped from her berth in Southampton and steamed into the chill waters of the Solent. Simon watched from the ship's rail as the shoreline of England receded into the mist. He knew that his forthcoming journey to America would prove as crucially important to his company's future as had his father's journey from Russia to England forty years earlier. As the great four-funnelled liner, sister ship to the ill-fated *Titanic*, steamed down the Channel to Cherbourg, and then on into the wintry Atlantic, Simon began his final preparations for the busy schedule of visits and meetings awaiting him in America.

In later years he would recall how the journey had come about. In 1923, he had confided his concern on the Woolworth competition to a distant American relative who was visiting Britain that year on business: 'I told him of my anxieties. How did others in the States counter this opposition? Could the businesses live side by side and still prosper? He encouraged me to make my first trip to the States and promised to give me introductions to some firms who were operating successfully despite the same competition.' The relative, a German, owned music publishing businesses but was also involved in New York's financial scene. He would provide Simon with some very useful contacts in the retailing industry.

The seven-day Atlantic crossing allowed Simon to consider family matters and, inevitably, Zionism. His friendship with Weizmann had grown even closer; Simon was a confidant of the Zionist leader and a sounding board for his future plans. Two years after the publication of the Balfour Declaration, Simon had accompanied Weizmann as his secretary to the 1919 peace conference at Versailles, where the Zionists presented their case to the council of ten for the establishment in Palestine of a Jewish national home under a British mandate, responsible to the League of Nations. One of Simon's duties was to carry the draft of the Zionist's case and application, which had been prepared in London, to Paris to show it to the British representative, Major Ormsby-Gore. Simon was discouraged when Ormsby-Gore, having read the draft, told him to tone down the Zionists' case. However, after some minor alterations to the draft, representatives of the Great Powers agreed to a British mandate in Palestine based on the principles of the Balfour Declaration.

Israel Sieff had earlier accompanied Weizmann as his personal assistant to Palestine as a member of a commission to determine how the Declaration's principles could be turned into reality. Simon and Israel had agreed that the task should fall to Israel; 'Simon was not a natural leg-man,' he was later to write, 'and did not have the temperament of a personal assistant; and we thought I could get on better with our leader than he could.' Simon came away from Paris further impressed with Weizmann's genius as both a statesman and a negotiator. As Israel later noted, 'In 1919 Weizmann behaved as though he had a great Jewish state behind him. In fact all he had, if he had been asked to show, was his handful of Manchester friends – Scott, Sidebotham, Sacher, Simon Marks and me!'

The British delegation to the 12th Zionist Congress in Karlsbad, Czechoslovakia, c. 1921.

As Simon recalled these epic events during his voyage to America, the British mandate over Palestine was just five months old. Since the end of the war in 1918 the country had been placed under British military administration. During that period, consideration of the Arab's growing resentment had caused the principle of the Balfour Declaration to be gradually eroded, including a reduction in the area of land originally designated for a Jewish homeland, a reduction which the Zionist executive, including Simon Marks, had to accept.

The British were becoming enmeshed in a confrontation between the Jews and their Arab neighbours. Many of the senior British officers stationed in Palestine knew little of the Declaration, with its implicit message of British approval for the formation of a Jewish homeland; others were pro-Arab, and some simply anti-Semitic. To the Arab population of the area, the gradual Jewish immigration appeared threatening and overwhelming. Riots broke out; both Jews and Arabs died. To Simon, who had always sought an accommodation between the two communities, the breakdown in the relationship was tragic. He was, nevertheless, still absolutely convinced that the Jews had no choice; the

Elaine Marks, Simon's youngest sister, in a photograph taken soon after the family moved to London.

The wedding of Elaine Marks and Norman Laski (right) in 1926. Neville Blond (later her second husband) was best man. Michael and Hannah Marks, Simon and Miriam's children, were attendants.

First WIZO executive meeting in London, c. 1920. Among those present are Miriam Marks on the far left, Miriam Sacher on her left and Rebecca Sieff fourth from left.

only home for the new generation of Jewish refugees produced by the Great War was in Palestine.

As the millions of Russian Jews were now shut off from their Western kinsmen by an anti-Zionist regime, and Polish Jewry now barely survived under an anti-Semitic government, the enormous financial requirements for the development of a new nation fell squarely on the shoulders of Jews living in the West. Simon was in the forefront of the fundraising.

One of the prayers of supplication on the Day of Atonement says, 'prayer, penitence and charity avert the evil decree.' While Simon expended little energy on prayer and penitence he embraced to the full the Jewish concept of charity. His enthusiasm and his refusal to accept nothing less than the maximum an individual or an organization could afford was irresistible. As he boasted in later life, 'Rich men run when they see me coming!' He also wrote, 'Jews discovered that giving on a scale that would have shocked them before was within their means and added a zest to their lives.'

Simon's journey to America in 1924 also provided him with a restful interlude to mull over the affairs and interests of his family. His main considerations were for his sisters, particularly the unmarried Tilly and Elaine. Both, he considered, would without his protection fall into the clutches of money-grabbing adventurers. Indeed, Tilly was protected so effectively by Simon that she did not marry until well into her fifties, and even then Simon protested over her choice of husband.

Elaine, the youngest and fourteen years Simon's junior, now lived almost permanently in London with her brother and Miriam. In 1926, at the age of twenty-four, the effervescent Elaine would marry Norman Laski, a member of a wealthy and influential Manchester Jewish family. The avuncular and self-effacing Laski was not Elaine's first choice of husband but, as she wrote, 'within the confines of Simon's dictate, Norman offered the only practical escape route into adulthood.' Her true love, the good-humoured

Rebecca Sieff, described by her husband Israel as 'a beautiful woman with the mind of a dynamic man'.

and urbane Neville Blond, Norman's cousin, was rejected by Simon because of his somewhat dubious social activities – Blond's amatory adventures in Paris and England after World War I were well known. In the 1940s, to Simon's chagrin, Elaine would divorce Norman Laski and marry Neville Blond.

Simon's eldest sister, the forceful and dynamic Becky, thwarted by Simon's opposition to her joining the company, had since her youth devoted her enormous energies to the women's movements. She founded the Women's International Zionist Organisation (WIZO) in 1920 and was also greatly involved in the suffragette movement. She was, in the words of her husband Israel Sieff, 'A beautiful woman with the mind of a dynamic man'. Miriam, married to Harry Sacher, was considered by many to be the cleverest member of the family and was a woman of style, character and beauty. Examining a portrait of herself painted by Augustus John, she delightedly exclaimed to friends that the

The interior of the Eastbourne store, 1925, an Aladdin's cave of kitchen utensils, bowls and buckets.

artist had portrayed her exactly as a prostitute. During the 1920s she moved with her husband to Palestine, where he practised for many years as a barrister.

As he disembarked from the *Olympic* in New York City, Simon might well have considered himself a fortunate man. He was wealthy, in good health, enjoyed a pleasant family life and in Zionism he had found an all-absorbing activity outside his business interests. Now, he wryly considered, all that was necessary to complete his happiness was to discover the way forward for his and, as he still regarded it, his father's business. Many a less-experienced businessman would never have realized that Marks & Spencer even needed a change of direction; this was a measure of Simon's strategic powers. The company was after all still progressing – turnover in 1924 was £764 thousand in comparison with £554 thousand in 1919. But as Simon was uncomfortably aware, the generally available merchandise he was selling could very easily be sold by rivals at lower prices; without a major policy change the business would either fail within a few years or be absorbed by a larger organization.

Simon apparently confined his first American business trip to the eastern seaboard, where he was delighted with the candour of the American retailers:

'I did not realize how open and helpful and generous American businessmen were in showing strangers how they operated . . . they seem to have no secrets from one another – so different from in England where everybody seemed to have secrets from everybody else. The men I met were happy to be of service to me – a complete stranger. After my first experience I made it my business to visit the United States as often as I could.'

In his notes he referred to only one American retailer by name – Sewell Avery of Montgomery Ward. On a later business trip, Avery advised Simon on the role of technology in obtaining the correct goods, and his prominence in Simon's account might

The staff of the Bishop Auckland store, 1928.

be due to Simon's admiration for the American's tough stance on matters of business principle. For instance, in 1944 Avery defied a presidential order to requisition a division of Montgomery Ward considered by the government as essential to the American war effort. Refusing to co-operate with the order, Avery was carried bodily from his office by the military police.

The American trip resolved many of Simon's business problems. He later wrote: 'In New York I met many men in the business. I learned many new things. It was my first serious lesson in the chain store art.

I learned the value of more commodious and imposing premises. I learned the value of checking lists to control stocks and sales. I learned that new accounting machines could help to reduce the time formidably to give the necessary information in hours instead of weeks. I learned the value of counter footage and how in the chain store operation each foot of counter space had to pay wages, rent, overhead expenses and profit. There could be no blind spots in so far as goods are concerned. This meant a much more exhaustive study of the goods we were selling and the needs of the public. It meant that the staff who were operating with me had to be re-educated and retrained.'

Simon's paternalistic personnel policy never inhibited a ruthless pursuit of excellence in the business. He went on to write: 'The old loyal guard had grown up with me with their limitations. Some were able to grow, others were not.' He had vigorously scored out this last sentence from his notes (written in 1960), perhaps ominously indicating that several loyal 'others' did not long survive his new regime.

The Marks & Spencer board minutes of 2 April 1924 noted that, 'The Chairman gave an exhaustive report upon his visit to America and his views on the general aspect of the large stores.' The desirability of operating large stores was but one of three major concepts that Simon brought back with him. First was the principle of restricting selling prices to a maximum of five shillings, the equivalent of the one dollar maximum price Simon had seen used in the United States. This would reintroduce a pricing discipline, which had been lost when the penny price point was abandoned during the First World War. Second was the realization that larger stores allowed a more effective display of merchandise, particularly clothing, plus the efficiencies of relatively fewer staff and the ability to accommodate the increased number of customers that Simon could foresee in the future. Third was the introduction of a system of sales and stock recording, subsequently called 'The Checking List System'. Coupled with the use of office machinery, the system allowed the rapid compilation of sales information on a detailed line by line basis. Consequently,

The Bradford store, c. 1930; the larger interior allowed for more effective displays and for gangways to encourage customers to walk around inspecting the goods on the 'island' counters.

in comparison with the previous antiquated system of quarterly returns, a much more efficient control of the flow of merchandise from the manufacturer to the store became possible. Simon, through this third innovation, had begun the introduction of information technology into the day-to-day running of the business. It is a tribute to the efficiency of the Checking List that it was in operation for over sixty years, before its replacement in the late 1980s by a computer-based system.

Israel Sieff was always convinced that Simon had formulated the basis of the lessons brought back from America at least two years prior to his visit. He simply needed the confidence of seeing them work in practice to ensure their application to Marks & Spencer. Putting these concepts into practice was a long and intricate task. The introduction of the Checking List system was, however, relatively easy to implement, and the development of larger stores was already tentatively in hand before Simon's departure to America. The greatest problem was the introduction of a five shilling maximum selling price.

Marks & Spencer, like the majority of large retailing organizations, bought the bulk of their merchandise from wholesalers. These intermediaries between the manufacturer and the retailer offered a valuable service to smaller shopkeepers, providing them with a credit system as well as enabling them to select from a large range of goods in a multiplicity of sizes and colours in the wholesalers' warehouses. Simon was aware that though some of the wholesalers' ranges might fall within his new requirements, the bulk of the merchandise he intended to sell did not exist and would have to be specially created. If the wholesaler could not provide the merchandise he required, then there was only one source that he could turn to – the manufacturers themselves.

Marks & Spencer had bought a small proportion of their merchandise directly from manufacturers since Tom Spencer had introduced the practice at the turn of the century. But to convert the entire merchandise range of a large retailer to a 'manufacturer only' basis was virtually unknown within the retail world. The wholesalers, quite understandably, became very concerned with this undermining of their valuable middleman position. Manufacturers were warned that if they dealt directly with retailers they would be struck off the wholesalers' lists. Nevertheless, Simon knew that his way forward for Marks & Spencer was the only way possible – he needed to be able simply to tell the manufacturer what the customer required. No intermediaries were necessary.

The search for ranges of merchandise into which Simon could incorporate his concepts of value and quality had narrowed down to family clothing – merchandise which neither Marks & Spencer nor Woolworths were selling to any great extent. The demand for clothing and in particular women's wear, had been growing since the end of the First World War. Before, the clothing of the average working-class man and woman consisted primarily of heavy, unstyled working clothes, plus a single 'Sunday best' outfit, which when it wore out would in turn be used for work.

The war brought a realization to working women that having earned reasonable money in munitions factories and similar war work they had sufficient surplus income to spend on the more attractive, fashionable and lighter-weight garments sported by their middle-class counterparts. This requirement for a higher class of clothing continued after the war, producing a growing light-clothing industry in the Midlands and London. The influence of the cinema, advertising and the popular press also allowed people to see the clothing of others, factors which were creating a demand that Marks & Spencer, if suitably adapted, could effectively satisfy.

Simon had two unique advantages not available to his commercial rivals. Firstly, in Israel Sieff he had a loyal and highly able collaborator with the relevant practical experience in textiles gained through his family business. With his diplomatic skills Israel would tackle the problem of convincing clothing manufacturers to supply merchandise direct to Marks & Spencer. Unfortunately for Simon, up until 1926 Israel's primary responsibility still lay with his family's business; he was only a part-time director of Marks & Spencer. Simon's second advantage was his relationship with the diplomat/statesman and chemist Chaim Weizmann. In return for Simon and Israel's friendship, Weizmann advised his friends on new scientific developments that could benefit Marks & Spencer, including the emergence of man-made fibres well before such materials were even approaching the production stage. According to Israel Sieff, Weizmann urged his two friends not to see themselves as 'mere shopkeepers'. Instead, Israel wrote, 'We came to regard ourselves as a

The new superstore Plymouth, opened in 1929; at 8,800 square feet, it was nearly seven times larger than the Penny Bazaar that it replaced.

kind of technical laboratory. We felt it was one of our functions to provide our suppliers with expert technical information about the new materials and processes which the advance of technology was making available.'

However, in the immediate aftermath of Simon's American trip Marks & Spencer had no suppliers who could use such technical information. It was Israel who made the first breakthrough. After many unsuccessful attempts to convince clothing manufacturers around the country of the benefits of supplying Marks & Spencer direct, he achieved his first success with the well-established clothing firm of Corah of Leicester. It took him four separate visits to convince the firm it would be in their best interests in terms of long production runs and guaranteed contracts to deal direct with Marks & Spencer. The first three times he was shown the door. Finally, on his fourth visit, Corah's production director accepted (under conditions of top secrecy from his own chairman) an order for 1,000 dozen men's socks. Corah, from whose Saint Margaret trademark Marks & Spencer would derive its own St Michael brand name in 1928, remained a supplier to the business for sixty years, until its absorption by another company. After Israel's fourth visit there, Simon was waiting for him at St Pancras station; 'Simon,' he said, 'I think we have made a breakthrough.' And a breakthrough it certainly was.

Following Corah's lead, other manufacturers decided to throw in their lot with Marks & Spencer and defy the powerful Wholesalers' Association. The new suppliers realized the benefit they would achieve from the price economies of scale and reduced staffing numbers – fewer sales representatives are needed when the majority of the production is destined for but one customer. 'We built up a unique relationship with our suppliers,' Simon later wrote, 'For their part they were to study new methods, new machines and the rationalization of their buying of raw materials at the most appropriate times. For our part we assured them of a ready market which was expanding year by year....' The concept was beautiful in its simplicity and typical of Simon's strategic thinking. If the manufacturer then took advantage of lower mass-production costs by accepting a modest unit profit, and Marks & Spencer did likewise, then the ladies' dress, children's shoes or men's pullover, sold at Marks & Spencer for five shillings, simply could not be bettered for value by any rival who bought his stock from a wholesaler. Not only would Marks & Spencer and its manufacturers benefit but, most importantly, so would the customer. It was the perfect scenario, in which the customer, the retailer and the manufacturer would equally benefit.

The super stores that would display Simon's new ranges were, when he returned from America, virtually still only concepts – expensive concepts. To create a nationwide chain of such stores would be vastly expensive and beyond the capabilities of a private company to finance. For instance, in 1925 the Birmingham store's site alone cost £30,000. Bank loans, mortgages and overdrafts – Chapman would have been appalled at their size – would no longer suffice. Only a public flotation could provide the necessary funding to fulfil Simon's business ambitions.

During his trip to America Simon had evidently discussed his plans and financial requirements. In August 1924, after his return, he received a letter from a Mr Germain, the financial entrepreneur – and a distant relative – who had initially suggested the trip, saying that he had 'come across Mr Merrill of the firm Merrill Lynch and Company who is an old acquaintance of mine', and had suggested to him that a merger between the Kresge Company (a large US retail chain) and Marks & Spencer might be possible. Mr Merrill apparently 'thought very well of the idea'. Mr Germain continued, 'The main

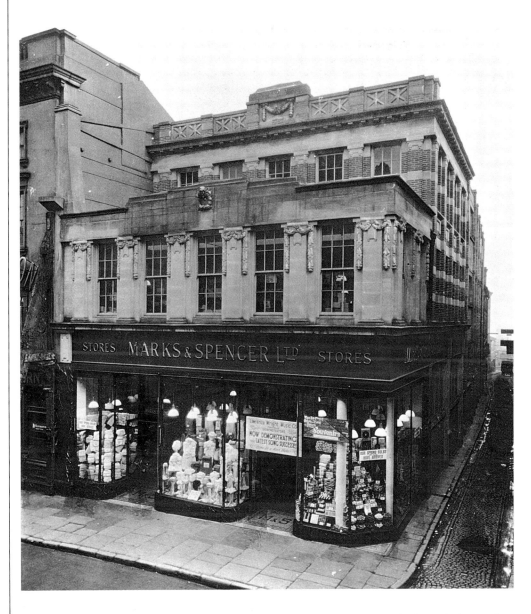

Marks & Spencer, Birmingham; the site was acquired at a cost of £30,000 in 1925, the rebuilt store opening in 1927.

point in my mind is that you and your shareholders would greatly benefit by such a transaction, provided the shares were sold in this country.'

Simon did not take up the American offer. Instead, he requested the Marks & Spencer company solicitors to provide him with recommendations on how to secure further capital without affecting the position of the company's existing shareholders. The solicitors, Arthur Benjeman and Cohen, replied that the 'best way of accomplishing the matter would be to form a new company to acquire the assets of the old company.' In July 1924 Simon, and solicitors representing the Marks and the Spencer family interests, were given board approval to begin negotiations with appropriate issuing houses. The first firm Simon approached, the British Foreign and Colonial Corporation, rejected the proposition – a decision that it doubtless later regretted. For eighteen months the public flotation hung in the balance until the Prudential Assurance Company, via an associated organization, the Industrial Finance & Investment Corporation Ltd, agreed to handle the issue.

The idea was that a new public company should acquire the entire assets of the private company; the consideration to be paid in ordinary shares. Working capital, however, would be obtained by a separate issue of preference shares to the public. A problem arose, however, when members of the Spencer family, with one exception, insisted that they would only accept cash for their near half portion of the private company's shares, not shares in the new company. Only the shrewd Agnes Spencer had sufficient confidence in Simon to deny herself an immediate cash profit and instead accept her payment in the form of new public company shares: 'I follow whatever Simon does', she declared. The Marks family and their friends bought the remainder of the Spencer shares for £8 each.

Sir George May, the secretary of the Prudential, now insisted that his company would guarantee the issue of the preference shares only if the Prudential was allowed to purchase 5,000 shares of the private company's original 33,000 shares. While this demand reflected a vote of personal confidence in Simon Marks by one of the nation's great financial institutions, it frightened the remaining shareholders. They realized that if allowed, this 15 per cent shareholding by the Prudential could soon be reflected in the same proportion of shares in the new company. And with this substantial toehold in the new company, it would prove a simple matter for the Prudential to obtain overall control of Marks & Spencer at a later stage. The entire Marks family, apart from Simon, opposed the deal, as did Simon's fellow directors, John Luther Green and Alexander Isaacs, plus the Company Secretary, Ernest Berry.

With such opposition it was only natural that Simon felt misgivings in allowing the Prudential any share in the equity. However, the Marks & Spencer company solicitor, Saville Cohen, considered that Marks & Spencer could only *benefit* from having a major financial institution as a shareholder. He convinced Alexander Isaacs to reconsider his opposition. Isaacs then spoke to Simon, who then, in Saville Cohen's words, 'rang me up one day from his home in Frognal saying, to use his own expression, "The scales have fallen from my eyes – get on with the matter at once."'

The deal was made; in June 1926 Marks & Spencer became a public company. Financially, Simon did very well from the flotation. His package included 60,000 shares in the new company, plus share options, which would in the early 1930s make him a millionaire. To safeguard the Prudential's financial interests, Sir George May had two of his nominees appointed to the Marks & Spencer board. But Sir George's interest in the new company extended well beyond the basic business level. The tall, monocled financier and Simon were to become close personal friends. As Simon later recalled:

'The Prudential had large monies to invest and were looking for businesses which required capital and which appeared to hold out promise for future success. Sir George was not only interested in such businesses but particularly in the men who were directing them. I had many conversations with him and he would encourage me to discuss with him the possibilities of our new approach. He would say: "Let us dream awhile – give our imagination full play. Business is always a risk and a speculation and without vision no business can hope to succeed. You will get there slowly by your own work – but I can help you telescope time!"

And so it was. He would provide the finance required and our task was to provide the programme of work as outlined in our discussions.'

May's natural flair for finance, developed since 1887 when as a sixteen-year-old junior clerk he first joined the Prudential, would subsequently be at Simon's disposal until his death as Lord May of Weybridge in 1946. It was at May's suggestion that Marks & Spencer, in 1928, introduced non-voting shares to protect Simon's unique style of management

The Chairman Simon Marks at his desk.

and control of the company from outside interests – Simon still had vivid memories of his battles with Chapman!

Despite Simon's unassailable position as Chairman of Marks & Spencer, he became aware that he was quite alone on his pinnacle of success. His other colleagues on the board, though loyal to him, did not have his concept of where the future of the company lay. In 1926 two of his directors were financial nominees of the Prudential – Richard

Simon Marks with fellow directors (left to right) Israel Sieff, Norman Laski and Alexander Isaacs, 1926.

Norland and Sir Harry Verney – a third, John Luther King, was basically an administrator. Norman Laski, Simon's brother-in-law, had only recently joined the company and had little retailing experience; the shrewd and capable Alexander Isaacs was now in poor health. Only Israel Sieff offered Simon the sympathetic and intellectual friendship within which, in Israel's words, Simon 'could tell his dreams without feeling inhibited by a sense of vulnerability'. To Simon's delight Israel agreed to join him as his Vice-Chairman, on a full-time basis for a trial period of one year. That one-year trial would eventually lead to a partnership of thirty-eight years.

Israel was surprised when on his first day at the firm's Head Office in Chiswell Street

97

Simon and Miriam Marks dressed for a costume party in London.

he found that Simon had installed a desk for him in his own office. Israel queried that the dual arrangement might encourage him to bother Simon with too many questions. Simon eagerly responded, 'No, you must be in here because I *want* you to ask me questions. That is exactly what I want.' To Harry Sacher, their mutual brother-in-law, Simon wrote soon afterwards that with Israel ' . . . I feel I have at last that intelligent co-operation which is essential if we are to get the uttermost out of our business.' Sacher later remarked of his two brothers-in-law that they constituted 'A board which did not have to rely upon formal meetings but was in permanent session.'

Between them the two men hammered out the company's basic principles, principles which would continue to serve Marks & Spencer well over the coming years. Simon wrote, 'Our discussions day in and day out, week in and week out, our work together resulted in our evolving a policy and a philosophic outlook on business and life which are the foundations of our business.' Coupled with their concept of retailing as an exercise run for the mutual benefit of the retailer, the customer and the manufacturer, came the realization that codes of conduct which were inherently morally good would prove equally good for business, hence the introduction in the 1930s of the company's welfare scheme, which by removing some of the pre-welfare state concerns of the company's personnel produced an immensely loyal and enthusiastic workforce.

Simon's introduction of the company's new set of working principles was therefore not entirely altruistic. He acknowledged in later years that good working conditions produced good work from his staff. He was also aware that by insisting on a 'Made in Britain' policy, not only were his goods manufactured close to his stores, but their production details could be easily worked out in English. It also meant that fully employed British clothing workers might well spend a significant proportion of their pay in Marks & Spencer. There was a final benefit to Simon and Israel. An established set of guiding rules, successfully instilled in the minds and souls of their executives and staff, would allow the two men some freedom; a certain 'hands-off' approach.

Israel Sieff, in a television interview recorded over forty years later, said that he and Simon had '. . . wanted to limit our responsibility and labour. We wanted to have a good time too. When things had reached a stage that we could go home at 6 or 7 p.m. and go to the theatre and carry on our public work . . . ', then the two men would be satisfied. But, Israel continued, 'We could only find the leisure time when we were satisfied that everybody was doing what we wanted them to do to produce that particular item.'

It was during this period that Simon 'sanctified' his father. He decided that a trademark would give a seal of authority, so to speak, to his goods. He warmed to Corah's 'St Margaret' and, with their permission, gave permanency to the memory of his father Michael. On 5 November 1928, 'St Michael' was registered under the Trademarks Act and soon appeared on a range of textiles, toys and other goods. In 1940 the first food item appeared under the brand, and by the time Simon first referred to it in a chairman's speech in 1949, it had become the recognized guarantee of quality that it remains to this day.

During the 1930s, when profit before tax exceeded £1 million for the first time (1935), the business had become for Simon his personal Aladdin's cave. It was his own toy, his love – 'There is nothing relating to Marks & Spencer which does not interest me,' he often said. His eye for detail was legendary. When in 1930 the expansion of the company required a move of Head Office from the City of London to larger premises at 82 Baker

'St Michael', the company's brand name and symbol of quality and good value, was registered as a trademark in 1928. This example dates from 1932.

RIGHT 82 Baker Street, the home of Marks & Spencer's Head Office from 1931 to 1958.

BELOW RIGHT Textile testing laboratory at Head Office. Specification buying, the ordering of merchandise in precise detail in advance of production, was developed during the 1930s.

BELOW A design department at Baker Street, 1930s.

Street, Simon, together with the company architect, surreptitiously visited other firms' new London offices to inspect the latest fashions in fittings. It was he who selected such items as the ornamental lamps that guarded the entrance to the new Head Office as well as the design of the office lifts.

Simon would tour the buying departments in the new Head Office with a posse of directors and executives in tow. New lines would be presented to him by the departmental selector and merchandiser. Simon would inspect the garment closely, examining every aspect from the styling and finish to the buttonhole stitching, after which he would pass judgement on the line's suitability. Comments such as 'It's not our business' or the much more serious 'Why are you trying to ruin my business, young man [or lady]?', would immediately consign the merchandise to oblivion. The offending item would either never be sold over a Marks & Spencer counter or if it was, would be discreetly dispatched to a store in a part of the country seldom visited by Simon.

Every opportunity was taken to preach the importance of quality and value. In 1935 Simon had installed in Baker Street the company's first textile laboratory, to ensure the quality of the made-up fabric and to allow the technologists to specify to the manufacturers in detail the quality required. It was a source of great pride to Simon and Israel that as retailers they did not merely sell the products of others but they also acted as production engineer, chemist and laboratory technician, the combined efforts of whom produced the final offering to the public of quality finished goods.

Once, on a visit to the Head Office toy buying department, Simon was shown a sample model car. The merchandiser proudly declared that following negotiations with the manufacturer, he had managed to reduce the price of the toy from 3s 11d to 2s 11d. Simon slowly turned the toy over in his hands. 'Last year', he commented, 'this car had a base plate. Now there is only a body shell and four wheels.' 'Er, yes Sir,' the young man instantly responded, 'That is how we managed to get the price down.' There was a moment's pause, then Simon disdainfully tossed the toy on to the merchandiser's desk: 'I imagine, young man,' he said quietly, 'if we take the wheels off as well, we can get the price down to 1s 11d.' The model subsequently appeared with wheels, body shell *and* base plate.

One of Simon's proudest moments came in 1930 with the opening of the company's first major store in London's West End. Located on the corner of Oxford Street and Orchard Street, near to London's famous Marble Arch, it consisted of the ground floor and basement of Orchard House, a recently erected office block just across the road from the giant Selfridges department store.

From its opening day 'The Arch', as it would become known to generations of the company's staff, became Simon's 'personal' store. Indeed, it was he who had forced through the acquisition of the site against the advice of several of his fellow directors, when even Sir George May of the Prudential felt the time was still too early in the company's development for such a large and expensive undertaking. Simon insisted: 'Even if it never makes a profit, it will be a good advertisement for the business.' On the opening day, 5 November 1930, a reporter for a group of Midland newspapers toured the store: 'I wandered today around one-third of a mile of counters laden with good things in the latest Oxford Street London Store,' he wrote, 'quite lost in amazement at what I saw. It was the price and value of the goods which made me wonder. Nothing was over five shillings and yet similar goods in many shops would cost at least two or three shillings more.'

At the time of its opening the Arch was the company's largest store by area, though not in turnover. Situated less than ten minutes' walk from Simon's spacious and luxurious office in Baker Street, the store would receive a visit from the Chairman at least once a day. Simon would question the store's manager on all aspects of the store's operation – its sales performance, stockholding and progress, new ranges and individual lines. Once in

The company's first store in London's Oxford Street, which was opened at No. 458 in November 1930. Known as Marble Arch, it became the flagship store, visited by Simon Marks at least once a day when he was in London.

the store's public café bar, Simon exhaustively interrogated the manager on its progress: 'What variety of cake sold best yesterday?, How many sandwiches did you sell?, How many customers did you serve last week?, How many cups of coffee and tea did you sell?' And so on. Eventually, more than a little annoyed perhaps at the manager's ability to answer all his questions, Simon floored him with, 'so you sold 520 cups of tea yesterday? How many were with sugar?'

Simon's continual presence at the Arch ensured that only the company's fastest-selling and most attractive merchandise was allocated to the store. Similarly, the store's management team was specially selected by the company's personnel department for their ability, brightness and presentable manner. The store manager was well aware that Simon in effect managed his store for him. At any other branches, the store management would routinely adjust the display area devoted to a particular department, depending on the

BELOW Advertisement for the opening of Marble Arch, where no item of merchandise cost more than five shillings.

ABOVE Window display of toys and sports equipment at Marble Arch, 1930s.

ABOVE RIGHT The Marble Arch store after its first extension in May 1932, which had become necessary after only thirty months trading.

season and on the departmental takings. At the Arch these minor moves would have to be referred first to Simon for his approval. His daily visits to the store continued virtually until the day he died and over the years his manner in the store did not vary.

Richard Greenbury worked in Marble Arch as a young Departmental Manager in the late 1950s and accompanied Simon on his tours around the departments. Greenbury [now Sir Richard and Chairman of Marks & Spencer] recalls:

'Simon could be a forbidding man; his manner was extremely blunt and direct. He did not mince his words and always said exactly what he thought. It was obvious to me that he was not only the Chairman of the business but also its owner and proprietor. Probably the most frightening thing about him was that he was always right!'

Simon's addiction to his business did not prevent his enjoyment of outside interests.

His early love of sport gradually evolved during the 1930s into a passion for tennis. In his enthusiasm for the game he hired professional players to play against him. When the professionals were not available, Simon would coerce members of his own family into playing. Gabriel Sacher, his sister Miriam's son, was on one occasion chairing an important meeting in Baker Street when he was summoned to the telephone. Simon came on the line. He wanted a partner immediately for a game at the company's private tennis court in nearby Maida Vale. Despite Gabriel's protestations of the importance of his meeting, Simon insisted on his partnering him.

Horse racing also took Simon's fancy. At Tattersalls' Newmarket sales in October 1935, two fillies were purchased for him at a cost of 900 and 700 guineas respectively. He subsequently named them Caldo and Fredo (Italian for hot and cold). By 1937 he had added a further two young horses to his string – Haganah (named after the then unofficial Jewish self-defence force in Palestine) and St Michael. Sadly, despite the efforts of his capable trainer Sam Darling, and top jockeys including Gordon Richards, Simon's horses did not win a single race for him.

By December 1938, following his business policy of clearing poor lines, three had been sold off. Only Haganah was retained on the insistence of Simon's daughter Hannah. After the Second World War, Simon achieved greater racing success with his horse Penny Stall, but later sold it as, it was said, he was concerned that when the horse's winning streak came to an end, many of the company's staff who loyally backed it would suffer financially!

The emergence during the early 1930s of Simon's insistence on the quality and value of merchandise, and, whenever possible, on its purchase from Britain, was gradually changing the company's cheap, Penny Bazaar image with the public. Indeed, the opening of a handsome 'Marks & Sparks' store in a town's high street became a source of civic pride. The company was becoming as much part of the urban scene as the town hall or the local police station.

Marks & Spencer was acquiring the status of a national institution. Her Majesty Queen Mary confirmed the company's new-found prestige when she wrote in her private diary on 18 March 1932: 'Went at 10.00 a.m. to Marks & Spencer in Oxford Street to see specimens of goods made in England.' *The Times*, in an article the following day, noted that during her half-hour tour of the store the Queen:

> '. . . bought an Axminster rug for five shillings, a leather handbag for 1s 11d, a willow pattern teapot for one shilling and a 21-piece tea service for six shillings.
>
> There was no formality about the visit and Her Majesty walked through the shop with Mr Simon Marks, the Chairman of the Company. She constantly asked him about the origin of various articles and expressed her pleasure at the great number which were of British manufacture.'

As the Queen made her purchases, a member of the store's management team, following behind the royal entourage, discreetly placed on the ranges where the Queen had bought an item a small ticket proclaiming 'As bought by Her Majesty'. At the end of the tour, when the Queen had departed with her party, Simon turned to one of his executives, Willie Jacobson, and with glistening eyes murmured 'Well, Willie, that wasn't bad for the son of a pedlar!'

In later years, when defining his attitude to the wellbeing of his staff, Simon wrote that one of his tenets was to 'take out of business life its asperities and needless hardship – in other words if possible, to make life happier and more secure for those with whom we were associated.' From the beginning of the company's history when Michael Marks had installed a simple form of heating in his covered market stalls, there had always been a desire by the management of the company to improve the staff's working environment. In America, Simon saw that daring investment in better working conditions made for more efficient, as well as happier, employees. But as so often happened, the trigger necessary to start a revolution in staff welfare was a comparatively trivial incident.

While visiting a store in the north of England with Simon, Israel asked an assistant to pack something up for him. Simon glanced up at the clock and saw that the girl's lunchtime had already begun. 'Don't you start on that,' he said, 'or you'll be late for your

ABOVE Simon enjoyed sport. He is seen here as a member of the Head Office cricket team in June 1930.

OPPOSITE By the 1930s Simon had developed a passion for tennis, and he enjoyed playing with professionals as well as family and friends. From left to right: Danny Prenn, Edmond Burke, Simon Marks and his nephew Marcus Sieff, chairman of Marks & Spencer from 1972 to 1984.

ABOVE The interior of the Birmingham store, 1933, showing the brightly lit displays and wide range of merchandise.

RIGHT Blackpool's Bank Hey store, opened in 1939, an impressive building on a corner site. Between 1931 and 1939, 162 new or rebuilt stores were opened.

lunch.' 'Oh,' she said, 'that's all right, it doesn't make any difference, I won't be having any lunch.' 'Not have any lunch?', Israel replied, 'It's very bad for you going without food in the middle of the day. Why aren't you having any lunch?' 'I can't afford it,' she answered. The two were shocked, as Israel later wrote:

RIGHT AND BELOW Window displays from the 1930s: printed dresses in a variety of styles and sizes all for five shillings; and jumpers and gloves.

'That night we sat up late talking and came to the conclusion that even if we paid wages which in the majority of cases were as generous as general trading conditions could stand, there would still be cases in which individuals, possibly because they had extra demands being made upon them at home – brothers and sisters out of work, an invalid brother, or some problem of that kind – would so wish to scrape the last farthing to take home that they would go without their lunch or tea.

There was only one thing that could cope with this, and that was to provide a hot meal at a cost so low that an employee would have to recognize it as uneconomical not to pay for it and eat it.'

The seeds were thus sown for a revolution in staff welfare, but Simon and Israel needed someone to mastermind the changes.

While enjoying a dinner party one evening in 1932, Simon was suddenly accosted in front of the other guests by his immediate neighbour, one Flora Solomon, who castigated him for the substandard conditions he provided for his staff. As Mrs Solomon recounted in her memoirs, *From Baku to Baker Street*, Simon was stunned by her rebuke and in particular her parting shot – '. . . it's firms like Marks & Spencer that give the Jews a bad name.' Simon appears to have been impressed by this blunt approach, however, for he recruited Mrs Solomon to take charge of the company's staff welfare. Thus would a remarkable woman, daughter of a multi-millionaire Russian banker and former mistress of Alexander Kerensky, the liberal Russian prime minister, join Marks & Spencer and with Simon's blessing develop what was probably the finest staff welfare scheme in industrial Britain. She was awarded the MBE for her services in 1946.

RIGHT Staff restroom, 1930s.

ABOVE A staff cloakroom, spacious and immaculate.

Others with perhaps less flamboyant backgrounds were also joining the company at this time. Simon was anxious that the company should remain a family-run operation, and ensured this by bringing a new generation of the family into the firm. During the 1930s Israel's sons Michael and Marcus joined the company, and their sister Judith worked for a while as a staff manageress. Teddy Sieff, Israel's younger brother, joined Marks & Spencer in 1933. During his first months Teddy lived with Simon so that the master could personally impart to the company's latest recruit the principles and essence of the business. Harry Sacher's son Michael joined the business in 1939, followed by his younger brother Gabriel just after the end of the Second World War in 1946.

Simon's own children, Hannah and Michael, never worked for the company for any length of time, despite Hannah's particular aptitude for business and for figure work. Her younger brother Michael, a highly intelligent young man whose artistic and bohemian interests lay – to Simon's regret – outside the Marks & Spencer world, had developed an almost love-hate relationship with his father. In later life the much-married Michael was to declare that he was a 'fugitive from a chain store'. He would on one occasion horrify his father at a family dinner party when Simon and Israel asked his opinion of a Marks & Spencer cake, served as a dessert, which they were tasting and examining in great detail. To Simon's mortification, Michael loudly declared, 'Look – I'm sorry, I just can't get interested in Devon Splits.'

Tragedy struck the Sieff family in 1933 when Israel's son Daniel, a scientifically-minded boy of eighteen, was found dead in his bedroom at the family home near Regent's Park. The coroner recorded a verdict of suicide despite the family's insistence that young Daniel had accidentally asphyxiated himself while experimenting with ropes and knots. He had, his parents claimed, so much to live for; the day after his death he was due to depart for Palestine to study at the Hebrew University.

Daniel's death devastated the family. It was Chaim Weizmann who suggested to the

The Daniel Sieff Research Institute, named after Israel and Rebecca Sieff's youngest son who died at the age of eighteen, opened in 1934 in Rehovot, Israel. It later became the Weizmann Institute of Science and enjoyed world renown as a centre of excellence.

grieving Israel and Rebecca, as the three walked in London's Hyde Park, that if they wished to commemorate Daniel's memory in a meaningful way they might consider the funding and building of a suitable scientific institute in Palestine. Simon, the Sachers and Daniel's parents liked the idea and, as a result of their generous contributions, the Daniel Sieff Research Institute opened in Rehovot, southeast of Tel Aviv, in April 1934. Simon gave the opening address and Weizmann subsequently served as the Institute's first president. In later years it evolved into the internationally famed Weizmann Institute of Science.

There survives a long and fascinating letter written by Simon on the Lloyd Triestino liner *Ausonia*, on which he was returning to England from the opening of the institute. Addressed to Israel Sieff and dated 7 April 1934, it gives a rare insight into the inspiration that Simon drew from his visit and the great deal of thought he was already putting into the Zionist cause: 'What we thought might be possible only after generations of hard work is rapidly developing à vue de l'oeil.' He marvels at the development of Hebrew and the fact that meetings were being conducted in a long-dead language: 'Will I ever be able', he writes, 'to understand or express the simplest of my views in my own maternal tongue? Can I still make the effort to be intelligible to my own people?' He goes on to write about the expertise being shown in agriculture in 'decades instead of as with other peoples centuries'. 'What splendid human material, heroes all', he enthuses, adding 'I am trying to write to you soberly without exaggeration but I find it difficult.'

Michael Marks, Simon's son, born in 1920. The arts appealed to him more than retailing.

He exalts in the beauty of Jerusalem, deplores the suburban, ever-growing Tel Aviv and takes pride in 'the settlers of our one thousand family scheme at Beertuvia, our present southernmost point, destroyed in 1929, today larger, more virile, trading with Arab as well as Jew.' He then refers to the opening of the Daniel Sieff Institute (which Israel and Becky did not attend, perhaps because they would have found the experience too painful), and talks of the role that it would play, both in the realms of science and in helping Palestine. The institute, he says, 'has been a labour of love for Chaim. It is a great memorial for our lost son.' He then mentions sitting down to a traditional Passover meal at the King David Hotel – 'a lukewarm affair conducted by a Minister whose spiritual home was Brooklyn.'

April 7ᵗʰ 34

LLOYD TRIESTINO

p/c Ausonia

My dear Israel, It needed a journey of this kind to re-vitalise me + to inspire a mind which was becoming jaded. Palestine has been a ferment in which ideas, ideals thought are boiling over. So much development is taking place there that at the moment it is difficult to obtain a correct perspective of what is happening. I believe the last few months have been strategically more important than all the previous years since the Balfour declaration. What we thought might be possible only after generations of hard work is rapidly developing à vue d'oeil. The most outstanding thing the development of Hebrew strikes one as miraculous. The meetings of the AC are held entirely in Hebrew although in many cases it

An extract from Simon Marks's letter to Israel Sieff, written while on board the *Ausonia* after visiting Palestine in 1934.

In the early 1930s, Weizmann had fallen from grace within the hierarchy of the World Zionist Organisation. In 1931 he had been voted out of office as president as the delegates considered that his pro-British stance (in view of what they regarded as Britain's friendship with the Arab side in Palestine) was inappropriate for a person in his position, especially at a time when Arab/Jewish rioting had resulted in over 250 deaths. Simon was present at the congress in Basle when Weizmann, replaced as president, angrily left the hall. He accompanied his friend and mentor, who was accused by an American delegate of having 'sat too long at English feasts'. At the next congress two years later in 1933, Weizmann was, despite his absence, nominated to head the department for settlement of German Jews.

The creation of the new department was necessitated by the viciously anti-Semitic policies of Adolf Hitler, appointed Chancellor of Germany in January 1933. Within weeks of his taking office, Hitler's brown-shirted storm-troopers were hounding Jews in the streets and enforcing a boycott of Jewish-owned businesses, and in particular Jewish shops and stores. Suddenly Jews, whose families had lived in Germany for generations and who regarded themselves as totally German in all respects, were pounced upon by the mob, beaten up, abused and forced out of business. Simon immediately retaliated by barring German-made goods from his stores. Orders totalling 25,000 dozen per week of artificial silk hosiery, then only obtainable from German sources, were cancelled. Simon transferred the business to Czechoslovakian factories, until that country too was trampled under the Nazi boot in 1938.

Simon's condemnation of all things German continued well into the early post-war period. He discovered that some wall clocks used in the company's staff canteens had been made in Germany. They were disposed of within a day. When German cameras, virtually the only ones available, were bought by Marks & Spencer for use in the sales promotion photographic department in the early post-war years, the staff discreetly removed the wording on the camera bodies indicating their origin.

In 1933, Simon realized that the Nazi persecution of the Jews was producing immigration problems vastly different from those which his father had known when he fled from Russia half a century earlier. In the 1880s Jews in their hundreds of thousands were allowed to enter into the United States, Britain and other countries with little restriction. These same lands in the 1930s were proving much more circumspect in their immigration policies. There were now barriers and immigration quotas. Even Palestine under British mandate – which in Zionist eyes should have allowed German Jews free entry – was restricting their admission.

Simon sprang into action. Within weeks of Hitler's accession to power he had, with a group of Anglo-Jewish communal leaders, formed the CBF, the Central British Fund for German Jewry. The main aims of the fund were to facilitate immigration from Germany and ensure that refugees who had escaped to Britain would not become a drain on the British exchequer.

Funds available in Britain were soon insufficient to meet the ever-increasing requirements of the rescue work. So, in January 1936 Simon, together with the Liberal politician Sir Herbert Samuel and Lord Bearsted, philanthropist and managing director of the Shell Oil Company, toured the United States to drum up further support and funds for refugees' relief. Between them the three men travelled thousands of miles making dozens of speeches and radio broadcasts to audiences in Chicago, St Louis, Philadelphia, Washington and New York. Despite their efforts, the appeal did not immediately produce the donations expected – American Jews were perhaps too far from Europe to appreciate fully the urgency of the situation.

A year later Simon returned to the United States on a follow-up tour, reporting on the fund's progress to the organizations he had addressed the previous year. In one of his speeches to American Jewish leaders he ended by declaring that the situation in Nazi Germany was a 'Dark Age' for the Jewish people. 'May the future Jewish historian', Simon declared, 'be able to write of our generation that we did not yield supinely to the resurgence of barbarism but dealt with every problem as it arose with courage and wisdom.' Simon was not a great orator; his delivery could be leaden and monotonous. But his speeches contained the nub of the matter and dealt simply and directly with his subject. Not content merely to coerce money from others, he led by example, personally donating over one million pounds to the CBF's funds.

Simon and his wife Miriam now lived in some splendour in Cleeve Lodge, a superb turreted and stuccoed house near Hyde Park Gate in the heart of socialite London. It was from here that Simon's daughter Hannah 'came out' as a debutante. Simon's position as a wealthy, generous and prominent businessman advanced him socially within the establishment. In November 1934 he was a guest at the wedding in Westminster Abbey of Prince George of Kent, son of King George V, to Princess Marina of Greece. In 1930, Prince George's royal relative, the debonair Marquess of Milford Haven, great-grandson of Queen Victoria, had joined Simon's Board of Directors. Similarly, Leo Amery, a Gentile supporter of Zionism and a future secretary of state for India, would join the board in 1936.

Simon's first public appointment – as a committee member on a commission to reorganize the egg and poultry industry in England and Wales – was announced in October 1933. Walter Elliott, the Conservative Minister of Agriculture and Fisheries, a personal friend of Simon, and perhaps due to their Zionist interests, wrote privately to him in September 1933: 'Will you help us by becoming one of the five committee members? I very much hope you will; the problems have their special angle in which you can be of more service than anyone else.'

Simon accepted. Fifteen months after the committee's first meeting in February 1935 their findings were published in a 200-page orange card-bound report, which was made available to the public at a cost of one shilling. By the time the report was published,

Simon's interest in the problems of the eggs and poultry might well have disappeared, for by then he had attended ninety-five formal meetings of the commission. The report, though generally well received by the egg and poultry industry, had its critics. The *Daily Express* commented on 8 February 1935, under the heading 'Marketing Madness': 'A headquarters staff. Twelve regional administrators. Two hundred packing stations . . . an

army of officials. Was there ever such a clumsy and fantastic experiment in bureaucratic socialism?'

Despite his charitable donations to both Jewish and non-Jewish causes, Simon remained an extremely wealthy man. He was also gaining recognition as a man of distinction and consequence who had established a business of national importance. In June 1939, to his delight, he was made an Honorary Doctor of Science by the University of London. According to the university's Honours Committee, Simon was: 'prominent amongst those who believe in the development of opportunities for education for those classes of students who for financial and other reasons can only avail themselves of the services of this University. It seems fitting that a degree should be conferred upon such an outstanding figure in the business world.' After thirty years Simon had reached educational parity with Israel Sieff, but sadly he would never enjoy the ceremonial presentation of his degree. Owing to the onset of war two months earlier, a report of the ceremony together with a eulogistic appraisal of his business skills, scheduled to appear in the university's *Gazette*, was cancelled.

On the eve of the second great war during his lifetime, Simon could regard his achievements with considerable pride. By the application of science and technology to the production of merchandise he had removed the so-called mystery from the buying of goods. He was now achieving the results that he and Israel had begun seeking twenty years earlier. In the thirteen-year period since the flotation of the company in 1926, a period which included the General Strike, unemployment and recession, the profits of the business increased twentyfold from £88,000 to £1,782,000.

Simon's philosophy that the basic function of industry and commerce was to make available goods and services to the public at affordable prices and thereby improve the

Simon was able to escape the pressures of company business with holidays abroad.
LEFT Simon and Miriam visiting the pyramids and sphinx, Egypt.
BELOW Enjoying the South of France.
BELOW RIGHT On holiday in the Alps.

general standard of life, was proving successful and profitable. In the view of Captain Victor Cazalet MP, who gave the customary vote of thanks at the company's AGM in March 1939, Simon, his colleagues and staff had taken Marks & Spencer far beyond '. . . merely a distributing agency; it has become a national institution playing a vital part in the economic life of the people of this country.' Simon would make a further significant contribution to the nation – this time outside Marks & Spencer – when, six months later, Britain found itself at war.

CHAPTER SIX

Serving His Country

A s the last few months of peace ebbed away, Simon ensured that his life's work, his Aladdin's cave, Marks & Spencer, was protected as far as possible from the effects of the imminent war. As Germany infiltrated and overran her Continental neighbours, Simon organized his company's defences. In March 1938, the time of the Anschluss, Germany's annexation of Austria, Simon appointed an expert engineer as the company's full-time air raid precautions manager to help, as he stated at the 1939 AGM, 'to organize and encourage our staff to learn to play their part in an emergency.' Some 4,600 members of staff – nearly 25 per cent of the total number – had by May 1939 been trained in first aid, fire watching and decontaminating duties. 'Each of our stores', Simon stated, 'has been organized to meet an emergency in so far as medical supplies, fire fighting and rescue equipment are concerned.' 'It was sad', he reflected, 'that business executives today had to concentrate a great deal of their time and thought on matters entirely unconnected with business.'

Despite the cost of the company's preparations for war, Marks & Spencer's profits after tax had risen to £1,782,000 in 1938–9, an increase of nearly £180,000 against the previous year. The company's 234 stores displayed a range of quality merchandise of which no single item cost more than five shillings. And as Simon proudly proclaimed, from the company's forty-four miles of countering more than 300 million individual items were sold to the public in a year.

Among the new stores – which were being opened at a rate of ten a year – was the company's second major store. Situated in the east half of London's Oxford Street, some half a mile from Marble Arch, it began trading in October 1938. Named the 'Pantheon' after the eighteenth-century indoor pleasure gardens that originally occupied the site, the new store had a magnificent black granite frontage which, marginally altered and extended over the years, has remained a prominent feature of this famous shopping street for over half a century. Simon was delighted with the trade press's description of the new Pantheon as 'the finest fixed priced unit in London if not England'. Preferring always to deal with family or people he knew and trusted, Simon employed as the Pantheon's designer Robert Lutyens – the son of the famous architect Sir Edwin Lutyens – who was married to Chaim Weizmann's niece Eve. He had previously worked on the interior refitting of Simon's house Cleeve Lodge, and Israel Sieff's sumptuous fifth-floor apartment in Brook House, Park Lane.

Three years after the Pantheon's opening, the store narrowly escaped destruction during the Blitz when a German bomb, smashing through the upper five floors of the store, finally lodged in the foundations, where thankfully it failed to explode. Apart from the Pantheon, over one hundred Marks & Spencer stores were damaged by enemy action during the course of the war, and sixteen were completely destroyed; over one hundred members of staff serving in the British armed forces were killed while on duty.

Trading continued, but Simon realized that not only would the survival of Marks &

Spencer be quite irrelevant if Britain were defeated in the coming war, but that with his Jewish background and activities, his own life would be at risk if Britain was successfully invaded. Indeed, his name had been cited in the rabidly anti-Semitic German newspaper *Der Stürmer* as one of the wealthy British Jews who were financially assisting their stricken brethren in Germany. Simon's sister Rebecca would be similarly pilloried in the same newspaper for her pre-war visits to Germany, where she had encouraged and assisted with the emigration of German Jews to the few countries who would accept them. More sinister still, Simon's name also featured, along with other members of his family, in the Gestapo's *Special Enemies List, GB*, a handbook prepared in 1940 by Hitler's secret police listing opponents of Nazism destined for immediate arrest following a German occupation of Britain.

Sensing that there could be no future for Marks & Spencer or himself in a Nazi-

ABOVE The Coventry store, which was bombed to the ground on 15 November 1940.

ABOVE RIGHT Temporary premises were found in a garage in Coventry.

occupied Britain, Simon sought an opportunity to serve Britain on a broader, patriotic front. One arose in 1937 when he was approached by Air Commodore Adrian Chamier, a retired World War I pilot who had enjoyed distinguished careers in the army, the Royal Flying Corp, the RAF and in the aviation industry. Chamier was then the enthusiastic and able secretary general of the British Empire's Air League, an organization founded in 1909 to increase the public's awareness of the importance of British aviation to both the country and the Empire. Simon was a member and had generously supported the League during the 1930s. In December 1937 he was invited, along with other businessmen, to a luncheon at Londonderry House, Park Lane, the London home of the League's President, The Duke of Sutherland. In a letter to Simon, dated 14 December (one week before the meeting), Chamier wrote: 'The Scheme we are going to discuss is really a very big thing indeed from an Empire point of view, and its contribution to our security and prosperity in years to come may be very great.'

Chamier intended to form an organization to attract aviation-minded young men into the Royal Air Force and provide them with some pre-entry training. Both the Army and the Royal Navy had such a cadet force, why not the RAF as well, he argued. The Air Ministry supported the plan and offered some financial assistance, including an allowance of 3s 6d per boy to each unit that passed certain proficiency tests. It was also hoped that the cadet squadrons would be financially supported by their local community; and the cadets themselves plus the Air League were expected to contribute to their expenses. A lump sum of £25,000 was nevertheless required to establish the central administration of the scheme, and to support over the next three years the expenses of ex-RAF officers who would tour the country to set up the fledgling 100-strong squadrons. Simon's role in funding the corps is recorded in the February 1951 issue of *Royal Air Force Review*: £7,000 [of the £25,000] had already been promised; Sir Simon there and then wrote out a personal cheque for the balance, and told the Air Commodore to return for more if it were needed.

On 7 April 1938 the plans for an Air Defence Cadet Corps were accepted at a meeting held under the auspices of the Air League. A working committee was immediately formed,

ABOVE AND ABOVE RIGHT A temporary store in the Lansdowne cinema in Sheffield, converted for the purpose and in use until 1952.

of which Marshall of the Royal Air Force, Sir John Salmond, was appointed Chairman and Simon Marks Honorary Treasurer. The majority of its early meetings were held in the panelled boardroom of Marks & Spencer's Head Office overlooking Baker Street.

Simon's contribution to the corps' organization was the great business acumen he brought to its financial and administrative problems. A booklet published in 1962 celebrating the twenty-first anniversary of the Air Training Corps (successor to the ADCC) noted Simon's insistence that the squadrons should not be solely dependent on a central fund: 'the fund would be there to help', stated the booklet, 'but he [Simon] insisted that the squadrons should be largely self-supporting and controlled by a committee of local citizens.'

By the end of the war, the corps had succeeded in its primary aim of attracting and pre-training youngsters for future service in the RAF. By 1945 over half a million young men had joined the ADCC and its successor the ATC; over 100,000 would subsequently enter the RAF. The earlier ADCC was a victim of its own success. Within a year numerous squadrons were formed. However, by 1941 both Adrian Chamier and Sir John Salmond, plus many of the corps' instructors had returned to the colours, which drastically reduced the time they had available for the corps' rapidly expanding activities. The ADCC soon began to suffer from a consequent lack of leadership and organization. The Air Ministry, not wishing to lose this invaluable pool of keen airmen of the future, decided as from 1 February 1941 to incorporate the ADCC within its main body, as virtually a junior branch of the RAF.

Air Commodore Chamier was transferred from his post in Balloon Command and appointed commandant of the reconstituted corps, which was subsequently renamed the Air Training Corps (ATC).

Two weeks prior to the reformation, Simon received a letter from the Air Ministry's Directorate of Training which read: 'My dear Marks, I write privately to convey to you my disgust at the complete lack of recognition accorded to your vital services as sponsor of the Air Defence Cadet Corps on the Corps being taken over by the Air Ministry.' The writer continued that he had brought Simon's 'invaluable aid' to the attention of high authority and trusted that Simon would get 'substantial recognition later on'. The writer, an RAF squadron leader and an aviation technical expert, who had previously served with Simon on the ADCC committee, ended with 'you may wonder why I feel so bellicose on this subject. My experience is that the wrong people invariably get the perks and I'm fed up with it! I know just how much we owe to you.'

The remains of the Plymouth store after bombing in April 1941. Sixteen stores across the country were completely destroyed by enemy action.

Within a few days of the squadron leader's unsolicited efforts on Simon's behalf, the Air Minister Archibald Sinclair personally wrote to Simon thanking him for 'the indefatigable help which you have given the movement as Treasurer' and inviting him to serve on the corps' Welfare Council and Board of Trustees. In a letter to Simon dated 7 February 1944, Adrian Chamier also acknowledged the corps' gratitude when he wrote 'Dear Mr Marks, you were the man who made the Air Cadets possible! On three separate occasions I have urged the Air Ministry to recognize this but . . . .' Though he enjoyed his centre-stage position within Marks & Spencer and also within his personal family circle, Simon was curiously reluctant to adopt the same stance in his outside activities. He never, for example, made an official inspection of an ATC squadron as he felt the young members involved might well be embarrassed by the inevitable 'Marks & Spencer Cadets' tag that would follow his visit.

Simon maintained his interest in the Air Cadets virtually until his death in 1964. A year earlier Lord Brabazon of Tara, President of the Air League, wrote to him for a donation towards the ATC's boxing championship. Perhaps forgetting or unaware of Simon's contribution to the corps' establishment he included in his letter details of their aims and activities. Simon gently chided the veteran aviator in his reply: 'As one of the founders of the Air Defence Cadet Corps which was later to become the Air Training Corps I am very happy to support this function ....' – and enclosed a £200 cheque.

Within months of the outbreak of war Simon received further requests for his services. On Friday 6 September 1940 he was chairing a meeting of the London and South Eastern Area Production Board. Two months earlier Harold Macmillan, then at the Ministry of Supply, had pressed Simon to accept the board's Deputy Chairmanship. If Simon accepted, Macmillan wrote, '... you will be doing a real service for the country.' The London and

A temporary store set up in Pannier Market, Plymouth, and used until the original store was reopened after the war.

South Eastern Area Production Board was the largest of twelve similar organizations formed in early 1940 to streamline the production of war materials by providing a nationwide advisory clearing-house service for local industry. Factories with over-full production programmes could subcontract their surplus work to other firms who had informed the area board of their spare capacity. Similarly, technical institutes whose students were now serving in the armed forces were guided by the board's technical officers into the precision manufacturing of parts for naval torpedoes, for example.

The boards maintained records of surplus plant machinery, allowing the emergency

transfer between companies of specialist equipment, and were also concerned with labour placement. At a committee meeting held on 3 September 1940, Simon brought up the question of the placement of 376 unemployed refugees who were 'first class engineers and scientists', and enquired whether 'a sympathetic hearing could be given by technical experts to these refugees whose work would be of great value in munitions supply.'

The board meetings were held weekly at least during 1940 and frequently more often. The meeting on 6 September 1940 was held in Room 015 on the ground floor of Savoy Hill House, in central London, adjacent to the busy Strand thoroughfare. Apart from Simon in the chair, twelve members attended, including an engineer rear admiral from the Admiralty and representatives of the ministries of Aircraft Production, Supply, Labour and the Board of Trade. The minutes of this particular meeting record that Simon's main contribution was peevishly to request that the notes produced by a sub-committee 'might be improved without affecting the general purport' and that he had brought the unemployed refugees problem to the attention of the International Labour Department.

The significance of this particular meeting lay not in its content but in the date on which it was held. For virtually as the meeting was proceeding, six miles over Simon's head and those of eight million Londoners, a German high-altitude reconnaissance aircraft, almost invisible in the blue morning sky, was photographing the dockland area of London in preparation for the Luftwaffe's first massive air attack on the city. Thirty-six hours later Hermann Goering, supremo of the German air force, could justifiably claim in a radio broadcast that for the first time the Luftwaffe had 'struck at the heart of the enemy'. London had indeed been sorely wounded – 350 bombers with hundreds of escorting fighters had set the capital's dockland ablaze. When the aircraft returned to their Continental bases, they left 1,800 of London's inhabitants either dead or seriously injured in the debris. Fires that had been started during the afternoon's attacks cast a doleful glare into the night skies and served as beacons for the subsequent waves of German night bombers.

The towering clouds of thick smoke rising from the devastated docks and warehouses were easily visible from the roof of Simon's headquarters some eight miles to the west. Within the previous two weeks Marks & Spencer had also suffered its first war damage when German incendiary bombs clattered onto the roofs of the stores in Bradford and Swansea. The attack on London was on an altogether more massive scale.

Though Simon would doubtless have preferred the comparative safety of his Windsor country home he remained in London throughout the Blitz. With his Head Office still based in central London – although many departments had been dispersed to the provinces – and his public commitments centred on the capital, he considered there was no alternative. Nevertheless, he saw no reason to take avoidable risks. Cleeve Lodge, his Hyde Park Gate home, though of sturdy construction, would never withstand a Luftwaffe bomb. Nor with his domestic staff leaving for war work could the standard of living that he and his wife Miriam enjoyed be maintained. The obvious alternative was to move to

The Canterbury store, which narrowly avoided destruction in 1942 when adjacent properties were bombed.

a centrally located luxury hotel, preferably one within walking distance of Baker Street and of course, Marble Arch.

The modern, marble-clad Dorchester Hotel, overlooking Park Lane and the ack-ack guns in Hyde Park, fitted Simon and Miriam's needs to perfection. The Markses moved there early in 1941. Like similar establishments, this glamorous hotel had been seriously affected by food rationing, blackout regulations and the call-up. Now only accessible through a constricted main entrance, screened against bomb blasts by a wall of sandbags, it was suffering from wartime restrictions of menu and staffing; ration books were required for both staff and residential guests. Many of the hotel's British staff were now serving in the armed forces; while German and Italian employees had been interned. Yet for those who could afford its service, the Dorchester provided a very pleasant home in which to sit out the perils of wartime London. Apart from enjoying all the standard facilities of a top class hotel, the one great attraction for wartime guests was the enormously strong, three-foot-thick reinforced concrete raft at first-floor level which, surrounded as it was by the seven concrete floor levels above, virtually guaranteed the safety of those sheltering in the hotel's basement air-raid shelter (the Dorchester was never directly hit by a bomb during the war, so these defensive qualities were never put to the test).

Simon shared the hotel's facilities, including the shelter, with a cross section of London's rich and elite, such as Lord Halifax, the Home Secretary; the diplomat Duff Cooper; Somerset Maugham and the actors Lesley Howard and Cicely Courtneidge. He would have rubbed shoulders with senior Allied statesmen and military personnel, who in 1942 included the future commander of the Allied invasion of Europe, General Dwight D. Eisenhower. Most importantly for Simon, Chaim Weizmann also occupied a suite at the hotel.

Weizmann was at this stage in his life a deeply disappointed man. His faith in Britain as the fair-minded administrator of the Palestine mandate had been virtually destroyed in 1939 with the publication of *The MacDonald White Paper* – Malcolm MacDonald was Britain's Colonial secretary – which declared Britain's future policy in Palestine. The Paper called for a very restricted Jewish immigration into Palestine for five years, at the end of which immigration would be at the discretion of a permanent Arab majority. In addition, a savage restriction on land purchase – the Jews' only legal way to acquire land – was decreed. In Weizmann's eyes the White Paper virtually annulled the Balfour Declaration, Britain's commitment to a Jewish homeland.

Britain had imperative reasons, however, for this apparent favouring of the Arab cause: at a time when the world was plunging towards inevitable war, she could not afford to add the Arabs, plus their fellow Muslims in the Indian subcontinent, to a list of potential enemies. As soon as the White Paper was published Weizmann orchestrated a campaign of critical letters to the press with a rallying of Zionist support – both Jew and Gentile – within Parliament. Despite the vehement rejection of its terms and the parliamentary opposition of Winston Churchill and Marks & Spencer's director, Leo Amery, the White Paper was passed into law – however, the Conservatives' usual Commons majority of 250 was reduced to 89.

These were sad days indeed for Simon. His fund-raising for resettling the victims of Nazism made him well aware of the fate of those refugees, afloat in derelict 'death ships' off the coast of Palestine, who were refused entry by the British mandate authorities due to the restrictions of the 1939 White Paper. In a speech later in the war to a group of American Zionists visiting Britain, Simon declared: 'We would be

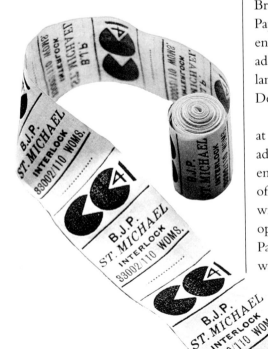

A roll of utility mark labels used for stitching into clothing during the war; the National CC41 mark indicated that the garment complied with government standards. Known as utility standards, they had been established with the help of Marks & Spencer technologists.

ENTER HERE

To-day's MENU

A neat, hygienic café bar installed during the war to make use of the space left by the shortage of clothing.

less than human were we not to express our profound sorrow and our wounded feelings at the needless hurt we have sustained. We would be unjust if we were to confuse those responsible for this outrage with the great British people whose ideals are still justice, mercy and charity.'

Despite his growing public responsibilities and fund-raising activities, Simon's major involvement still centred on 'The Business'. As in pre-war days, he would still on Saturdays visit his favourite stores, where, with homburg hat jauntily perched on the back of his head, he would probe the sparse displays of wartime 'utility' clothing, questioning as always the store staff on the sales and stock situation. Recently recruited staff did not always recognize him. On one occasion in 1941 he entered a utility room at the rear of the Staines store, and was happily puffing away on his cigarette when he felt a hand grab the collar of his jacket, turn him round and dump him outside in the goods reception yard. To Simon's consternation the store's new warehouseman then shouted at him, 'Can't you read, the sign says "No Smoking"'!' The poor man almost fainted when the store manager, shortly on the scene, fearfully introduced him to Simon Marks: 'Give this man ten shillings rise' (a considerable sum in the early 1940s), ordered Simon, 'I make the rules – that does not give me the right to break them!'

By this time, public café bars had been installed in many stores to fill the space caused by the lack of clothing. The national CC41 utility clothing mark, now prominent on nearly all the company's merchandise, denoted that the garments complied with wartime standards of quality – indeed Marks & Spencer technologists, in co-operation with government scientists, had been responsible for devising many of the rigorously enforced national specifications.

Many of the company's pre-war improvements in clothing standards had been brought about by a refugee from Hitler's Germany. In 1935 Eric Kann, forced from a senior technologist position in the German chain store Schockens by the Nazis' anti-Semitic laws, was visiting London on the way to a new job – and a new life – in the United States. Simon Marks showed him around the Marble Arch store and confidentially asked Kann his opinion of the merchandise: 'Shmutters!' [Yiddish for rags], was Kann's curt response, at which Simon promptly invited him to join Marks & Spencer '... and help us to improve it'. Eric Kann stayed, and in 1954 was appointed to the board of directors.

Even with the difficulties of wartime conditions, Simon still insisted on standards of the highest quality possible. Once, on meeting in a buying department a garment manufacturer who had produced some substandard merchandise, Simon's cruel tongue so mortified the man that, panicking, he dashed from the room through the first door available. Unfortunately it was the door to a built-in wardrobe. Even Simon ventured a grin when a few moments later the manufacturer sheepishly opened the door from the inside and stepped back into the room.

Simon would sometimes tolerate a certain amount of 'chutzpah' or cheekiness in those with whom he dealt. On one occasion, Ralph Salaman, the company's Air-Raid Precaution Manager, ushered into Simon's office the manufacturer of a line of phosphorescent exit signs for use in blacked-out stores. The man offered them to Simon at three shillings and ninepence each. Simon sized up the simple construction of the sign and sarcastically asked 'What's the three shillings for?' 'Well, Sir', the manufacturer replied, 'As a matter of fact, that's the profit.' Simon was so pleased with his reply that he promptly ordered twelve dozen for a trial. On Simon's instructions Ralph Salaman had to train the domestic staff of Simon's seven-acre country retreat, Titlarks Farm near Sunningdale, Surrey, in the technique of air-raid precautions. The staff were assembled on the lawn when, in Simon's words, '... Salaman stood up at the bedroom window, put the harness under his arms and dropped out of the window to the ground to show how simple it was....' Ralph Salaman recalled Simon's amazing ability to recognize the important among a mass of trivia, to cut through to the heart of the matter: 'He always seemed to jump on what was important. When he was not too tired and in a good mood, it was a joy to be with him. But he was a bit of a terror and people were frightened of him, including me.' Simon would often be 'awfully rude' to both directors and staff in Mr Salaman's presence – '... some people could never forgive him for the brutal things he sometimes said to them.'

During the war Simon delegated much of the day-to-day running of Marks & Spencer to Teddy Sieff – Israel's much younger brother who had been appointed to the board in November 1939. The younger male members of the founding family had joined the armed forces. Simon's son Michael served in the RAF. In the army, Israel's two sons, Michael and Marcus, both achieved the rank of colonel. Harry Sacher's two sons, Michael and Gabriel, were also commissioned – Michael becoming a major – and both saw action in North Africa. Simon's brother-in-law Norman Laski would provide a third colonel from within the ranks of the family.

A new branch was grafted onto the family tree in April 1941 when Simon attended the wartime wedding of his daughter Hannah to Alec Lerner, a Canadian army doctor serving with the dominion's forces in Britain. At the end of the ceremony, as the young couple left the West End synagogue, they walked under the raised batons of the officers of Captain Lerner's battalion. In post-war years Alec Lerner would become a Marks & Spencer director and be considered by Simon as his possible successor.

On a cold May night in 1940, an Allied merchant ship en route to America in a convoy off the southwest corner of Ireland was blown apart by a U-boat's torpedoes. The other ships in the convoy did not stop to pick up survivors; their orders were to steam on out of harm's way at top speed. From the deck of the surviving ship directly ahead of the stricken vessel, Israel Sieff, Simon's deputy, witnessed the fatal explosion. Some of his friends died in the shattered and sinking vessel.

The reason for Israel's mission to America with other British businessmen was to generate (at the request of the Board of Trade) American dollars by selling British goods and thus help to finance the war effort. He took with him samples of garment fabrics, fine cotton yarns and made-up clothing. At the same time he founded the Marks and Spencer Export Corporation, the company's first exercise in bulk exporting. In November 1940, the London *Times*, in an editorial headed 'An export policy experiment', commented favourably on Marks & Spencer's attempt to breach the high U.S. trade tariffs. Before the introduction of Lease Lend the British Treasury benefited by ten million dollars from the corporation's selling activities.

There might have been a second reason for Israel's presence in the United States during a period when Britain was in imminent danger from a German invasion. Indeed, Simon had already briefed non-Jewish members of the Marks & Spencer board to be prepared to take over the direction of the business if he and his family were taken by the Nazis. He may have further considered that Israel Sieff's presence out of harm's way in America might have still ensured some form of distant control of the business by the family should Britain be occupied.

Earlier in the war, as Simon recorded in the November 1939 board minutes, Israel had suffered a 'temporary breakdown in consequence of the strain of work under the existing war conditions'. A further reason for this breakdown may have been the repercussions of a love affair that would eventually cost him around £250,000 in out-of-court settlements. Simon, a great upholder of family morality, was embarrassed by the affair. He was also embarrassed when the innocent business activities in America of his friend and brother-in-law were questioned in Parliament.

In the early 1930s Israel Sieff was associated with the formation of PEP (Political and Economic Planning), an independent, non-partisan research and policy forming organization. The membership came from many professions and trades and included most shades of British political opinion. Israel contributed to PEP's well-researched reports on the social and economic problems of the day. In Britain, his policies and opinions would be considered middle-of-the-road; in the United States, certain right-wing politicians considered them dangerously radical. Nevertheless, in March 1942 he was invited by Leon Henderson a presidential economic advisor, via the British Embassy, to join the American Office of Price Administration in Washington in an unpaid capacity. His major duty was to share with American businessmen how Britain, after two years of war, was coping with rationing, price control and distribution.

Despite the almost universal appreciation of Israel's subsequent talks to gatherings of businessmen around the United States, certain Members of Congress considered his views were tantamount to converting the USA into a socialist state. Although Israel was questioned in Congress on his political views and those of the PEP organization, he would eventually emerge from the dreary affair with distinction as well as with a letter of commendation from the American Government. He decided to return to London – not however, before hostile reports had spread back before him to Parliament.

In 1943, a right-wing Conservative MP, Sir Waldron Smithers, raised a question in the House querying Israel Sieff's position in the USA and asking Anthony Eden, the Foreign Secretary, whether the American Government had 'asked that he [Israel Sieff] should be relieved of his work and returned to this country?' Israel had of course not been 'returned' to Britain, and Eden replied that he was aware of Israel relinquishing his American appointment, but understood that 'his work on the Committee was appreciated by his colleagues, who regret the loss of his services.' Another member of the House then succinctly summed up the exchange by enquiring, 'Would this Question have been asked about Mr Sieff if his name was Smith or Smithers?'

Simon similarly came under attack in November 1941 when Sir Waldron and a fellow MP raised a question in the House requesting information on 'the condition in which parties and entertainments were held for serving soldiers at the country home of Mr

The exterior of the Clacton store, destroyed by enemy action on 13 February 1944. It was the last store to be bombed by the Luftwaffe.

Simon Marks, the Chairman and Managing Director of Marks & Spencer Limited', and asking whether 'There was any leakage of information to the enemy at these alleged parties'. Simon was both hurt and offended by this slander, and in a press statement expressed his resentment that the questions should have been allowed in the Commons. He stated '. . . that he [Simon] was host to men on leave, most of them personal friends of his son-in-law who is an Army Officer.' The Secretary of War subsequently rejected the allegations, and Sir Waldron and his Rt Hon. friend made formal apologies to Simon in Parliament.

Simon's period as Deputy Chairman of the London and South Eastern Regional Board ended in June 1942. For the final eight months he had acted as Chairman due to the absence for health reasons of the official incumbent. Earlier that year he had also been appointed to the Citrine Committee, which had been commissioned, originally on the instructions of Lord Beaverbrook, to advise and recommend changes in the function and constitution of the Regional Boards. The committee's major recommendation, that the clearing centres which had so effectively pooled local engineering resources in London and the Southeast should be extended nationally, was a credit to Simon, who had championed their use. He regarded them, as he stated at his final Regional Board meeting, as 'not merely clearing centres for the exchange of capacity but . . . centres for a much wider field of production problems.'

Simon was understandably disappointed then, when following the Citrine Report's reformation of the Regional Boards, he was not re-appointed Chairman. He had thought there was much he could do to improve the board's effectiveness, including the gradual introduction of the efficient Marks & Spencer checking list system to the complex world of engineering production. The minister for production, Oliver Lyttleton, perhaps considered that a retailer, however eminent, might not be an appropriate leader in a production-oriented environment.

Victory window display in the Falkirk store, 1945.

Lyttleton personally wrote to Simon thanking him for his 'deeply appreciated' services, but Simon's feelings of rejection were apparent when in July 1942 he wrote to Harold Macmillan, then Undersecretary of State for the Colonies and the man who had originally invited him to join the Regional Boards in 1940 and who had also been moved on before the benefits of the Regional Boards had been established:

> My dear Harold Macmillan,
>
> I thought you would like to know that I have not been reappointed a member of the London & South Eastern Regional Board on its reorganization following the Citrine Report. In a minor degree to yourself, I now share the fate of a pioneer of a new system which has now received general acceptance.

Macmillan was sympathetic: 'I am very sorry indeed', he wrote, 'to hear that we have shared the same fate; but we have had the fun of starting the thing off, and that is really the only interesting thing in life . . . .'

In 1942 Simon added a further two public appointments to his list. Firstly, in April, he joined Sir William Jowitt's (later Lord Jowitt) advisory panel on Home Affairs, and later in the same year accepted the position of adviser to the Petroleum Warfare Department (PWD).

In 1940, the fall of France and the retreat from Dunkirk had removed the necessity for Britain to act as a major distribution centre for oil products to mainland Europe. Vast quantities of the surplus fuel had therefore built up in storage depots around the country. Could these stocks of oil and petroleum, the authorities considered, be used as weapons of war? The PWD was formed in July 1940 to research and produce just such weapons. The department's first products were 'Molotov cocktails' – simple glass bottles containing a pint of petrol and a cloth wick which, when ignited and hurled against enemy tanks, were blazingly effective. Then, during the months when Britain, bereft of the arms and munitions abandoned on the beaches of Dunkirk, was awaiting a German invasion, the PWD was practising, as a stopgap measure, the burning of thousands of tons of fuel oil

A Lancaster bomber taking off with the aid of the FIDO (Fog Investigation Dispersal Operation) system, which used the heat from two lines of flame to disperse ground fog at airports.

on Britain's coastal waters and her beach roads. In the stirring words of Geoffrey Lloyd, the petroleum minister, the concept was 'Flame all across Britain, ringing the coasts, spurting from the hedges and rolling down the hills. We will burn the invader back into the sea.' The department also devised the vicious flame-throwers which would prove so effective during the Allied landings in Normandy in 1944 and their subsequent advance into Germany. In the final days of the Second World War, Simon would have felt some satisfaction that the flame-throwers invented by PWD would burn down, destroy and help liberate the infamous concentration camps at Auschwitz and Belsen.

Simon's role in PWD was listed in the department's organization plan as 'Adviser to the Minister – assists general developments of the Department'. Simon saw this as an overseeing role – plotting the strategic needs of the department against its future plans and ensuring that the departmental 'goods' were produced as swiftly and efficiently as possible. He also refereed wrangles between PWD's diligent scientists and their sometimes impatient and demanding military customers.

Simon's appointment as adviser to Geoffrey Lloyd coincided with a directive from

Prime Minister Churchill to his petroleum minister, '... to find means to dissipate fog at aerodromes so that aircraft can land safely. Let full experiments to this end be put in hand by the Petroleum Warfare Department with all expedition. They should be given every support.' Too many air crews' lives were being lost when bombers, returning from raids over enemy territory often with dead engines and near empty fuel tanks, could not land at their home base due to impenetrable fog and were forced to divert or crash land. The development of FIDO (Fog Investigation Dispersal Operation) took just ten months from the Prime Minister's original request until July 1943, when a Lancaster bomber made the first successful trial landing on a fog-bound runway between blazing lines of burning petrol when visibility was down to 200 yards. The principle of FIDO was simple: the heat

ABOVE RIGHT Simon Marks (front right) visiting a Petroleum Warfare Department station in Hampshire, 1943, with a group which also included members of the Red Army.

given off from blazing petrol, pumped from nozzles in parallel lines of piping lying either side of the runway, caused water droplets, the basis of fog, locally to evaporate. A tunnel of clear air was thereby formed through which aircraft could safely land and take off.

Simon was administratively involved in FIDO's development from the beginning. He accompanied Lloyd and his chief executive, Major General Sir Donald Banks, to the test grounds at a variety of carefully chosen sites, including an enormous drained reservoir, some four miles in circumference, situated near Staines in Middlesex; a low-lying farm in Hampshire selected for its proneness to fog; and a converted ice-skating rink at Earl's Court. It was an exciting time: as Lloyd wrote to Simon in January 1944, '... you and I are bound together by the memory of the nights and dawns of mist and fog we shared in those days. I shall never forget them or the great contribution you made to so many aspects of our efforts to get this vital work started properly and quickly – and then keep it driving forward at maximum speed....'

In December 1944, FIDO allowed heavy bombers to take off from fog-shrouded bases in Britain and strike at the supply lines of Hitler's last desperate offensive in the Ardennes –

the so-called 'Battle of the Bulge'. The German Ardennes commander, Field Marshal von Rundstedt, later confirmed that these bomber raids caused the failure of this final major German attempt to reverse the course of the war. By the end of the war, over 2,500 aircraft and their 15,000 crew members had been safely brought to ground using FIDO.

PLUTO (Pipelines Under The Ocean) was perhaps PWD's greatest achievement. The energy and fuel requirements of the Allied armies as they fought from their Normandy

PLUTO (Pipelines Under The Ocean) being unreeled into the English Channel. Its purpose was to carry fuel to northern France, vital to the success of the Allies' D-Day landings in 1944.

beachheads in June 1944 across to Germany were colossal. It was PWD that co-ordinated the design and production of the complex system of pipelines which brought vital fuel from depots in Merseyside down to the south coast of England, where it was conveyed via under-the-Channel pipes to the French coast and on to the very borders of Germany. In total 575,000 tons of fuel were pumped 'under the ocean', often at a rate of over one million gallons a day. The consequent saving in tanker tonnage, subsequently transferred to the Far East had, in the words of the British Quartermaster General, 'a reaction which extended all over the World'.

Simon's involvement with PWD provided him with confirmation that research technology could solve the majority of the nation's production problems. It was a verification of Chaim Weizmann's pre-war discussions on the subject with Simon and Israel Sieff. An added bonus for Simon during his time with PWD was his meeting with Dr Paul Rosin, a German refugee scientist who had worked on the development of FIDO; after the war, Simon appointed him Marks & Spencer's Chief Scientific Adviser, a position he held for over twenty years. When Simon returned to his full-time duties at Baker Street, he displayed on his office desk a model flame-throwing tank, as a memento of his three-year attachment to one of the most effective (for its size) war-winning organizations ever created in Britain. In later years he would regard his work with the PWD as his most important wartime activity.

For much of the war, Marks & Spencer, with about half its pre-war staff away in the armed or auxiliary services, half its working area requisitioned by the government for food storage, and over half its Head Office departments dispersed to the provinces, was a mere shadow of its pre-1939 self. Even the two upper floors of Simon's Head Office in Michael House, Baker Street were now requisitioned for the clandestine Special Operations Executive (SOE) organization, a spying and sabotage group whose task, as defined by Winston Churchill, was to 'Set Europe Ablaze!' Simon never opposed any requisition order imposed by the government – several Marks & Spencer stores were indeed com-

The *Marksman* Spitfire, presented to the nation by Marks & Spencer staff in 1941.

pletely taken over by the authorities – and he actively encouraged his staff to become involved in the general civilian war effort. Neither did Simon neglect the company's men and women in uniform. Their service pay was made up to their pre-war company earnings and a company newsheet was mailed to them wherever around the world they were stationed.

Amid the daily problems of wartime life – bombing, blackouts, rationing and shortages – Marks & Spencer staff found time to knit thousands of garments for the Forces, to collect for a presentation to the nation of a spitfire aircraft aptly named *The Marksman*, and to organize emergency canteens for dockyard workers, bombed-out refugees and servicemen on leave as well as sharing their staff canteens with evacuee children. Flora Solomon, Head of the company's Welfare Department, was the driving force behind the government-sponsored British Restaurant system, which on a nationwide basis provided cheap, hot and nourishing meals for people disadvantaged by the war and for the children of working mothers. In 1940 the company's food technicians even evolved a nourishing canned soup called 'Blitz Broth'. In the same year a Royal Army Ordnance Corps (RAOC) unit was formed consisting of 225 Marks & Spencer men, who after training transferred to other RAOC units at home and abroad. The family feeling engendered within the business during wartime was sufficiently strong for a group of 500 volunteers to move en masse to a Ministry of Supply hostel for women workers at a Royal Ordnance factory in Radway Green.

Simon's Zionist activities during the war centred on extensive fund-raising initiatives

IN THE HOUR OF PERIL
~~MARKS AND SPENCER~~
~~LIMITED~~
EARNED THE GRATITUDE
OF THE BRITISH NATIONS
SUSTAINING THE VALOUR OF
THE ROYAL AIR FORCE
AND FORTIFYING THE CAUSE
OF FREEDOM
BY THE GIFT OF
SPITFIRE AIRCRAFT
They shall mount up with wings as eagles
Issued by the Ministry of Aircraft Production
1941

Plaque awarded to Marks & Spencer following the presentation of *The Marksman*.

for the Jewish national home. As Chairman of several appeals he realized the efficiencies of amalgamation, and after much discussion succeeded in creating a United Palestine Appeal, which in Simon's words would ensure 'that the experience gained by each of the major funds, if brought together and co-ordinated, could achieve even more substantial results for the great task which lies before us...' Simon would be elected President of the new fund, a position he held until his death. In February 1942 he had the painful task of telephoning Dr Weizmann, who was waiting on an airfield near Bristol for a plane to the United States, to inform him that a telegram had been received stating that his son,

Fortuna, a BOAC de Havilland 91 Albatross which crashed on 16 June 1943 while approaching Shannon airport. The passengers, including Simon, suffered only minor injuries.

Michael Weizmann, in Simon's words 'an intrepid valiant pilot of the Coastal Command of the RAF', was missing – alas, never to be found.

Simon's final wartime appointment was to the British Overseas Airways Corporation (BOAC) as Vice-Chairman. He accepted the position following the dramatic resignation of four BOAC directors – including the Chairman's in March 1943 – due to their disagreement with the Air Minister on plans for the future development of the corporation. Simon was one of three replacements made by Sir Archibald Sinclair, the Air Minister, in an urgent attempt to plug the gaps on the board. The appointments were not universally approved. The newspaper magnate Viscount Rothermere, in a House of Lords' discussion in April 1943, cuttingly criticized the new BOAC directors. One, he considered, was 'in his second childhood', the second's previous duties had 'merely been checking supplies'. 'Mr Simon Marks, at least,' Rothermere went on, '... has experience in commerce as owner or manager of a large chain of cheap stores; but I cannot conceive in his case what his qualifications are for going on the Board of British Overseas Airways. I dare say he was put down because he was considered a piece of sugar to cover the pill of the other two appointments. If that is the case, it must have been a wartime ration.'

Simon's new job did not require his special qualities as a retailer; it simply required a commonsense ability to see through the myriad problems facing a civilian aviation organization during a time of war. He helped to determine the course for the corporation's post-war airline operation and set his aviation experts the task of fulfilling it.

BOAC's wartime problems were manifold. Firstly, they lagged well behind the RAF in terms of allocation of new aircraft, air crew and base facilities. Secondly, their operations, due to the war, were over-complex. When Simon joined the board, the corporation operated ninety-one land planes and twenty-two flying boats, consisting of sixteen different types which operated from bases as widely separated as Durban, Baltimore and Bristol. Schedules were affected daily by the wartime conditions. In particular the corporation's unarmed aircraft flying to neutral countries, the USA and the Middle and Far East, were prey to enemy attack. In June 1943, for example, the British film actor Lesley Howard, was killed when his unarmed KLM Douglas DC3 airliner was shot down by German fighters over the Bay of Biscay while flying between Lisbon and Southern Ireland. Although Simon could do little to improve the corporation's wartime situation, he was able to indicate to his aviation experts the demands that the post-war world would make on British civil aviation in terms of routes, aircraft types and facilities required.

Simon's involvement with BOAC nearly saw the end of his business career – and his life. On 16 July 1943, the BOAC Albatross class airliner *Fortuna* was on its final approach to the Foynes, Shannon Air Base in the Republic of Ireland. On board the airliner were virtually all of the BOAC Board of Directors, including Simon Marks; their intention was to tour and inspect the corporation's facilities in Ireland. Suddenly, three-quarters of a mile northwest of the runway, and within sight of a waiting reception party, the aircraft dipped sharply and crashed.

Hilary Watson, head of BOAC's Irish operations, was first on the scene. With an axe from the fire rescue vehicle he hacked his way into the wrecked fuselage and found Simon shocked, petrified and still strapped into his seat. As Mr Watson attempted to release him Simon mumbled, 'Are you Hilary Watson?' As he dragged Simon from the wreckage, Watson responded, 'Mr Marks, this is not the time for formalities. This plane is about to explode like a bomb!' Despite severe damage to the fuselage, no one died or was seriously injured in the crash. Subsequent investigation showed that waterlogging had affected the aircraft's wooden structure; the Albatross class never flew on passenger service again.

At the time of the crash, Simon was aware that he was eligible for some form of recognition for his public activities. Lord McGowan, Chairman of Imperial Chemical Industries, and a personal friend of Simon, was discreetly lobbying for a knighthood on his behalf. The crash, together with an earlier letter from Lord McGowan to Archibald Sinclair, the Air Minister, detailing Simon's wartime contributions to the Air Training Corps and the Regional Boards, clinched the award. Thus, in July 1944, was Simon dubbed Knight Commander of the Most Excellent Order of the British Empire by King George VI in the Throne Room of Buckingham Palace.

It was just half a century from the year that his father Michael Marks, the illiterate immigrant Jewish pedlar, took Tom Spencer as his partner to set in train the retailing revolution that was to change Britain's high streets. It was as Sir Simon Marks that the pedlar's son would continue the retail revolution in peacetime.

Certificate of Employment in Essential Services in War, issued by Major General Donald Banks, showing that Simon was employed by the Petroleum Warfare Department.

CHAPTER SEVEN

The Final Accolades

n life, Angie, you have to cut out the dead wood – always cut out the dead wood.'
So murmured Simon to his friend Angela Fox as he pruned the azaleas in the grounds
of Titlarks Farm, his country home near Sunningdale, where Angela Fox and her
husband Robin – parents of the theatrical trio, Edward, James and Robert Fox –
were frequent guests of Simon and Miriam. Even in his garden, thoughts of the business
were never far away, and as he wielded the secateurs Sir Simon Marks may well have been
wondering how much dead wood there was in his beloved Marks & Spencer.

Situated in the heart of the Berkshire countryside, Titlarks was a farm in name only.
Acquired by Simon in 1942, the house was a haven of relaxation for him right up until
his death in 1964. It was set in seven acres of grounds, full of azaleas – Simon's favourite
plant – that produced a dazzling display each spring. A large, formal, circular rose garden
was set out next to the much-used tennis courts, and a broad-paved veranda extended
from the rear of the house down to the well-tended lawn, big enough and good enough
to serve as a championship croquet ground. Inset into the paved veranda, where the family
would sunbathe during the summer months, was a small flagstone carved with the
inscription, 'In the garden of happy memories, it is always summer.' The interior of the
rambling eight-bedroomed house, built in the early 1920s, was furnished with a flair made
possible by its owner's great wealth: the Impressionist paintings displayed there in 1961
included nine Renoirs, two Corots, two Utrillos and a Degas.

A similar taste in art and furnishings was also evident in the Marks's flat in Grosvenor
Square, where Simon and Miriam had moved after their wartime stay at the Dorchester
Hotel. It was Lady Marks's judgement and discerning eye that led to the purchase, often
at prices a mere fraction of their subsequent value, of many of the paintings, antique
furniture and Chinese works of art which adorned their homes. Miriam Marks was a tall,
striking woman with a commanding but not austere presence. An excellent hostess, who
retained well-trained staff at both Titlarks and Grosvenor Square, she prided herself on
being able to do anything her staff could do, but better. On one occasion when her cook
was suddenly taken ill, Miriam personally cooked and served dinner for thirty guests.

Simon and Miriam's guests at Titlarks were a varied group. Members of the family
mingled with senior industrialists, actors, Zionists, tennis players and personal friends. On
occasion, Lord Louis 'Dickie' Mountbatten would make an appearance. Simon had
sufficient regard for the dashing royal sailor to offer him a seat on the Marks & Spencer
board in 1961. Though Mountbatten, then Chief of Defence Staff, accepted the offer
following 'my retirement from the Navy', he was never actually appointed. Simon was a
plain eater, and breakfast with his house guests invariably started with his favourite dish –
two plump grilled kippers. Then at around 10 o'clock on a Saturday morning, he would
be driven in his Rolls Royce Phantom V, 'SM9', accompanied by one of his guests, to a
local Marks & Spencer store, probably the Slough or Staines branch. These stores, together
with Wembley, Windsor and Maidenhead, constituted the 'royal route' which Simon

Simon at his home, Titlarks Farm in
Berkshire. Behind him is a profuse display
of azaleas, his favourite plant.

A room at Titlarks hung with some fine Impressionist paintings.

took from Baker Street to Titlarks on a Friday afternoon. He would visit some of them on the way and again on the Saturday morning. All of them had managers handpicked to cope with the needs of the Chairman, who used his visits as the basis of his Monday debrief to his colleagues. Ernest Jones, the manager of Slough, was quoted as saying that the education he got was 'better than a university although more frightening'.

Although he had his favourite stores, Simon was passionately involved in the development of the whole chain. Sixteen stores had been destroyed in the war and many were severely damaged; because of government restrictions, rebuilding could not start until 1951 and it was not finished until 1957. Simon wanted to do much more than replace what was lost. He was determined to transform the whole chain, giving it 'a new look and a new character more in keeping with the specialized goods we are selling'. It was

BELOW The Windsor store, built in 1933, was one of Simon's favourites, often visited by him on his 'Royal Route' home.

RIGHT June 1962, Queen Elizabeth II visits Maidenhead and passes by another of Simon's favourite stores.

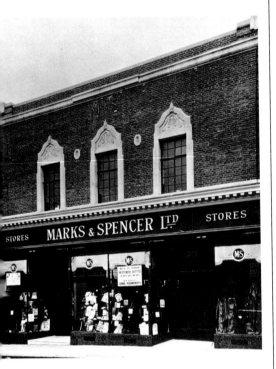

RIGHT The sales floor, Eastbourne, 1955, showing racks of clothing lined up with military precision. The original store on this site was destroyed by enemy action in December 1942; the new store opened in May 1955, with a sales floor of 12,500 square feet.

OPPOSITE, BELOW LEFT The new Coventry store, built to replace the one destroyed during the war. Opened in April 1954, it was 25 per cent bigger than its predecessor.

OPPOSITE, RIGHT Tidy, well-stocked, self-service food counters, Bradford, 1961.

also his mission to make sure that the style of the store was in keeping with the character of the high street in which it was situated, and he devoted some time and expense to this effort. Director David Susman remembers Simon saying, 'we are building a fairyland in the high street'; 'His eyes would glow', said Susman, 'and his face light up'.

In the ten years after the war, selling space was more than doubled from 136,000 square feet to 285,000 square feet, with the introduction of new, specially designed display fixtures and up-to-date decorative and lighting schemes. At the same time, Simon Marks ensured that great attention was paid to amenities for the staff – dining rooms, rest rooms and the like. Once, when touring a construction site, Simon needed urgently to use a toilet. He found the facilities provided for the building workers so appalling that he insisted that Bovis bring the catering and toilet facilities for their workmen up to the standards demanded in Marks & Spencer. This caused a minor revolution within the construction industry, and indeed it is still the practice for senior members of the company, when visiting suppliers, to ask to see the staff quarters. Simon's interest in working conditions may seem to suggest socialist leanings, but politically he was a Conservative – though his stance was towards the left wing of the Conservative Party. He would often declare: 'I learnt my regard for staff and their welfare from my father, Michael Marks, rather than from Karl Marx.' Israel Sieff's political stance, incidentally, while probably not dissimilar to Simon's, found room for a close personal friendship with Aneurin (Nye) Bevan, the Labour Party firebrand.

Britain's post-war Labour Government, with its plans for increasing nationalization, was not to Simon's taste, and he decided to look overseas to increase his business. South Africa attracted his attention and in particular the Woolworths (South Africa) Chain Store organization (no relation to the worldwide F. W. Woolworth Corporation). Max Sonnenberg, the company's founder, had a good business reputation and Simon, without

BELOW Israel Sieff, Aneurin Bevan (the Labour politician) and Simon Marks in conversation.

visiting the country but on the basis of photographs and reports, acquired shares in the company on behalf of Marks & Spencer. In December 1947 Simon went to inspect his new interest and was horrified at the standard of merchandise on display. According to Marcus Sieff's memoirs, Simon buttonholed Max Sonnenberg and said, 'You really can't offer these goods for sale; they should be given to the Bishop for his charity garden party.' At a second store, where his initial findings were confirmed, he said to Max, 'You can't even give this stuff to the Bishop for his garden party, you must burn it!'

Simon's sortie into South Africa would eventually prove rewarding for both firms. It also produced a further branch of the family when the capable David Susman, the young son of Max Sonnenberg's business partner Elie Susman, married Anne Laski, the daughter of Simon's sister Elaine. The link between the two businesses continues to this day. At the time of writing David Susman is Chairman of Woolworths (now Wooltru, South Africa) and a non-executive director of Marks & Spencer. Marks & Spencer still act as consultants to Wooltru. Marks & Spencer's advice is often sought, by companies, charities and government departments. It is a measure of the degree to which the business that Simon built up has so often led the field in certain areas.

Even before the Second World War ended, while many people were no doubt thinking of rebuilding their lives and their businesses, Simon Marks, the radical, the retail revolutionary, had already formulated his vision of the future for Marks & Spencer. In his Annual Review in March 1945 he called for 'a revolution in production and production methods to be achieved by cooperation between scientists, manufacturers and workers'. He spoke of science producing new raw material processes, with the creation of new synthetic fabrics and plastic substances. Two years later he referred to improvements in values, upgrading of goods, and setting standards. It is a philosophy which the current Chairman, Sir Richard Greenbury, describes as being 'in need of no change at all'.

Simon Marks was a champion of synthetic and man-made fibres. He knew that nylon and Terylene, with their unique, easy-care qualities, would have a far-reaching impact on the clothing industry. In 1954 he wrote:

> 'When some thirty years ago we entered the field of textiles, quality and beauty of garments were reserved for those of ample means. For the mass of the people, the clothing available was drab and of poor quality. The rise of the multiple shops displaying boots and shoes and all kinds of clothing produced by mass production methods brought about great social changes. Men, women and children changed over to more practical and attractive garments, cheaper in price and better in quality. It is not without satisfaction that we can say that Marks & Spencer had a prominent part in those social changes.'

Simon was being modest. He and Israel Sieff, in their fight for quality and value, had spearheaded the movement towards bringing good merchandise within the reach of the ordinary person, and his revolutionary zeal continued to set the pace. 'We are successfully pioneering new cloths,' he wrote, 'and collaborate closely with our spinners and knitters in working out new standards of quality always bearing in mind the end product and selling price to the public.' Simon's concept of his merchandise was extremely simple – all Marks & Spencer goods must offer quality and value to his customers. He was obsessed above all with quality. When he visited stores he would examine the merchandise closely, turning garments inside out to check the stitching, the lining, the finish . . . everything. Garments failing his critical inspection were brought back to Baker Street for a full investigation to ascertain what had gone wrong, and at what stage.

David Susman, chairman of Wooltru, South Africa. A non-executive director of Marks & Spencer, he married Ann Laski, daughter of Simon's sister Elaine.

Terylene skirts displayed in the Swansea store window, 1957. Simon was a champion of man-made fibres and knew that their easy-care properties would make them very popular.

His directors and executives dreaded Monday mornings. What had Simon brought back from his Saturday visits? The store manager would usually telephone the head office departments concerned as early as possible on the Monday morning, warning them of any faults that the Chairman had discovered. On arriving at the office Simon would take the offending item into the relevant buying department. If he was in a bad temper he would throw the garment onto the floor and accuse the people in the department of 'trying to ruin my business'. Otherwise the group executive, with technologists in tow, would be summoned to his office and interrogated on how such an 'abomination' could have occurred in a Marks & Spencer store. Simon would not drop the matter until he was completely satisfied that the source of the problem had been identified and dealt with. And he could be ruthless in such matters, but as his great-nephew, Marks & Spencer director David Sieff, recalls: 'Not ruthless in the search for power, but to improve the business'.

Simon's obsession with quality also extended to the behind-the-scenes aspects of his business such as hygiene and staff facilities. When he visited stores he would run the point of his nailfile down a join in the staff dining-room table checking for dirt or dust. At the Marble Arch store he discovered some dust on the wall behind a side counter; he immediately summoned a porter with a bucket of soapy water and a cloth. Then, to the embarrassment of the store's senior management, he took off his coat and jacket, and taking the cloth from the porter's hand proceeded to wash down the dirty area. When he had finished he put on his jacket and coat and quietly walked out of the store. That same day an urgent note was dispatched to all stores ordering them immediately to inspect and clean behind the counters. The lesson had been learned.

After the war, with consumer goods hard to come by, the company was still interested in pressing ahead with opening more of its café bars. In 1948 it had 107 in operation.

These were all to vanish by the early 1960s as ample quantities of good quality textile merchandise became available to fill the selling space more profitably. As clothing sales grew apace, so too did sales of food, which the company had been selling since the time of the Penny Bazaars. At the time it accounted for 25 per cent of sales; today (1993) it represents almost 40 per cent. The food division was to become the personal domain of Simon's nephew, Marcus Sieff, who together with Simon's son-in-law Dr Alec Lerner, as well as Dr Kann, Jan Lewando and Michael Sacher, Harry's son, was appointed to the board in 1954.

The Board of Directors, 1960. Clockwise from centre back: Sir Simon Marks, Israel Sieff, Teddy Sieff, Marcus Sieff, Michael Sacher, Harry Sacher, Norman Laski, Eric Kann, Alec Lerner, Michael Sieff, Jan Lewando, Wilfred Norris, Leslie Goldberg (Deputy Company Secretary) and Bruce Goodman. Nine of the fourteen were family members.

Despite the fact that selling food was not his first love, Simon's pride in his merchandise was just as strong. Alf Berman, then a vegetable technologist, remembers Simon once asking him why he had failed to put a new range of potatoes in Marble Arch. Berman's response that he didn't think the Chairman would find that appropriate drew the half joking reproof, 'the trouble with you is that you are a snob.' Soon after, Simon went into Marble Arch to find Berman arranging a display of potatoes. Having forgotten his instruction to introduce them, Simon said, 'my nephew is trying to turn me into a grocer and I am having trouble dealing with him. If you try to turn me into a greengrocer, I shall have no trouble, at all, in dealing with you!' However, when in 1959 he was taking Alan (now Lord) Sainsbury around a new Marks & Spencer store he could not resist showing off the new poultry department, pointing out a chicken which, he said, had 'a breast like Mae West'.

Naturally, food had to be cooked and prepared in scrupulously hygienic conditions, and Simon led the crusade for cleanliness. Goronwy Rees, in his book *The Multi-Millionaires*, explained:

'Everywhere he goes he asks questions, talks to people, looks into things, opens cupboards and refrigerators, like a very good battalion commander carrying out an inspection. He has, and his colleagues have, an almost fanatical interest in hygiene and cleanliness, as if everything must be impeccable and immaculate before it is good enough for the consumer or good enough for people to work in.'

Simon appointed his son-in-law, Dr Alec Lerner, to organize a campaign to achieve the highest standards of hygiene throughout the company. Dr Lerner produced a manual entitled *Hygienic Food Handling*, which filled a need outside the company as well as within,

Simon presenting a member of staff with a gold watch for long service, 1956.

and it was subsequently made available to numerous organizations, both commercial and otherwise. Marks & Spencer kitchens were held up as a shining example to hospitals and health authorities. The company received a letter from the catering officer of a large hospital saying that he had never seen a fly in their stores and would they please pass on the secret as he had 'not yet succeeded in that battle'.

Simon's approach to hygiene, as with everything else, was radical. In the 1950s the company sold ice cream, as did many larger stores, from a refrigerated cabinet at the front of the sales floor. Simon went into a store one day and discovered ice cream papers littering the floor. Appalled, he eliminated the product immediately, preferring to forfeit £1 million sales a year rather than see the stores spoiled by the public's untidiness. Another obsession was fire safety. In 1959, Marks & Spencer became the first retailer to introduce 'No Smoking' rules. This was seen by some at the time to be arbitrary and high-handed and likely to offend the public. It is of course now an increasingly accepted practice throughout retailing, not to mention cinemas, restaurants and public transport. In 1961 dogs (with the exception of guide dogs) were banned from Marks & Spencer stores to protect the displays of food.

Because he cared so deeply about the business, which until his dying day he regarded as 'his', Simon approached anything to do with it with a single-mindedness bordering on obsession. As a result, he took personally any action which he considered might damage the company, and to those who made mistakes he could be scathing in his criticism. Members of his family working in the business were not spared the lash of Simon's tongue, either. Marcus Sieff, a tough, dynamic individual himself, had many confrontations with his uncle: 'I received limited praise from him', Marcus writes in his memoirs, '... but plenty of criticism, much of it expressed in vigorous language. As a result I learned a great deal....' Similarly, director John Sacher recalls his late father, Michael Sacher, a nephew of Simon and later vice-chairman of the company, returning home pale and drawn after facing up to his uncle. Only Israel Sieff, Simon's lifelong friend and colleague, could do no wrong and was rarely criticized by Simon, in public at any rate.

Service rank was no guarantee of protection. In the early post-war days use of former ranks was still common. One member of Head Office answered the telephone with, 'Major Smith here'. 'This is Gunner Marks,' came the curt reply, 'Get down to my office!' Simon once asked a store manager if he was frightened of him and got the reply, 'Not frightened, Sir Simon – petrified!' There can be no doubt that Simon was also feared within the senior ranks of Marks & Spencer; his remarks could certainly on occasion be offensive. Once, on entering a buying department for a review, he found the Group Director and his Executive Assistant discussing the estimates. 'Ah!', observed Simon, nodding first to the Executive and then to the Director, 'the withered hand of the dead body!' When he realized, perhaps prompted by Israel Sieff, that he had said something particularly hurtful, a comforting arm around the shoulder and perhaps a conciliatory chat in his office would shortly follow.

In the manner of many great leaders, Simon became increasingly autocratic, even tyrannical, in his last years, perhaps because he was conscious of his own failing health and of his mortality. His criticism was not usually intended to be personal, however, and most of his victims were aware of this. In Simon's view, his intention was solely to ensure the protection of and progress of 'his' business – an approach he described as divine discontent.

Israel and Teddy Sieff listening to Simon.

The reverse of this confrontational attitude was most apparent in Simon's attitude to junior staff. He particularly enjoyed the company's annual Long Service Ceremony, when those with twenty-five and forty years' service were presented with gifts. Simon always ensured that the awards were made not only to Marks & Spencer staff but also to long-serving associates of the company such as the foreman from builders Bovis, who had worked on Marks & Spencer store contracts for over a quarter of a century.

To the youngest members of the family, mainly his grandchildren, Simon's confrontational manner was never shown – to them he was the perfect grandfather, loving and doting. He would often take the youngsters by the hand on a tour of a local Marks & Spencer store. A particular favourite was his eldest grandchild, Joel Lerner, who when accompanying Simon around the store displayed a genuine interest in what was going on. It compensated Simon to some degree for his son Michael's complete lack of interest in the affairs of Marks & Spencer, or indeed in Simon's other consuming interest, Zionism. Though Michael, now the second Lord Marks, worked in the company for some years after the war, his interests really lay in the worlds of writing and art.

Simon and Miriam with Joel Lerner, the eldest of their six grandchildren.

It is ironic that father and son were not closer, considering that whenever Simon's own father was mentioned, Simon would become very emotional. Having devoted his life to the work he inherited from the first Michael Marks it must have been an enormous disappointment that his son, also named Michael, showed no interest in carrying it on. Young Michael's conviction that his father had placed his business and Zionist interests before his parental responsibilities, together with Simon's obvious lack of interest in Michael's artistic leanings, caused a strained relationship between the two. In later life Michael would sadly recall that his father, though often kind and considerate, 'just did not understand the more ethereal type of person'.

In spite of his obsession with Marks & Spencer, Simon was able to relax. He would invite close friends, paying their expenses, to holiday with him in the South of France, usually at the Carlton Hotel, Cannes, where he would reserve an entire floor for the use of his family and guests. He would ensure that they received the best possible service by lavishly tipping the hotel staff at the beginning and end of the holiday. On occasion, rather than stay at a hotel, he would charter a motor yacht, usually the luxurious 500-ton, 170-foot-long *Radiant*, in which he would gently cruise along the Riviera coast, usually returning to Cannes harbour for the night. Simon was not a gambling man, and he made little use of the casino; his comment while watching a man losing heavily at the gambling tables was, 'better he should have given it to charity!'

Simon could never completely separate his holiday from work, however. On his return to Baker Street from a winter break on the Riviera he would bring back clothing that

RIGHT Simon and Miriam relaxing on holiday in Cannes with (left to right) Robin and Angela Fox, Lady McIndoe and Sir Archibald Hector McIndoe.

ABOVE The Carlton Hotel, Cannes, with Julian the head porter. Simon would on occasion reserve an entire floor for the use of his family and friends.

had caught his eye in the boutiques of Cannes. He would also return with some caustic observations: 'Gentlemen,' he once told his Board of Directors, 'I have been to France and I have found a new colour – it is white! Why isn't there any in my stores?' He was well aware during his holidays abroad, that some members of the board might take advantage of his absence. Once, on returning after a break, he asked a merchandiser in a buying department, 'What have the Brothers Grimm been up to while I have been away?' – this being his affectionate nickname for Israel and Teddy Sieff.

Though Simon enjoyed the recuperative qualities of a good holiday, he did not always recognize its benefits for his fellow directors. If their services were required, they would often be recalled from leave or have their entire break cancelled or postponed and, as Mrs Lois Sieff recalls, this was accepted by the victim without question: 'My husband, Teddy, just reacted without a word of complaint – that is what Simon wanted; that is what Simon got.' As Simon rarely attended the synagogue, even for the High Holy days, he could be less than sympathetic to observant members of staff who wanted time off so to do. Once he called for a lengthy report to be produced in the late afternoon prior to the Jewish New Year. He asked whether the executive concerned intended to take the following day off. The unfortunate man replied that he hoped to do so, to which Simon's comment was, 'Well you will have plenty of time to do the report today then.' Occasionally, when

Simon and Miriam enjoying the sunshine
at the Carlton, Cannes.

Simon and Chaim Weizmann
photographed in 1950, two years after
the birth of the State of Israel and
approximately two years before
Weizmann's death. Simon felt an
enormous sense of loss for the man who
had in some ways been a substitute father
to him.

taken to task by Jewish friends on his non-observant ways, Simon would concede that 'I sometimes think as a Zionist I have forgotten how to be a Jew.'

As a lifelong Zionist, Simon must have felt immense satisfaction when in 1948, at the age of sixty, he saw the state of Israel become a reality. With his mentor Chaim Weizmann as Israel's first president it seemed like a dream come true. In February 1949 Simon wrote to Chaim: 'How could Israel Sieff and I have realized when we first met with Vera and you that in some small measure we would share with you the Zionist work that would lead in our own generation to the realization of what appears to be the fulfilment of biblical prophecy.'

It is impossible to overstate the contribution made by Simon, Israel Sieff and Harry Sacher to the Zionist cause; virtually every study of early Zionism pays tribute to their joint commitment. As Chaim Weizmann himself wrote in his autobiography, *Trial and Error*, completed in 1948:

'Two young businessmen of great ability and a sense of social responsibility . . . Simon Marks and Israel Sieff, had been drawn into the movement. They were not Zionists at first, but they had heard me speak at one of the meetings, their interest had been aroused, and they wrote to me – this was 1913 – asking if they might come to see me and discuss the movement with me. From that time on we worked together, in a friendship which has meant much to me and to Zionism. For Zionism became increasingly the leitmotif of their lives, and they brought to it qualities of which we stood greatly in need.

They were young and energetic. They were practical, and they knew that work could not be done without a budget. They were not hampered by ancient Zionist dissensions, nor were their lives scarred by recollections of persecutions. They were jolly and they loved the good things of life. They helped me, in later years, to put some sort of organization into my rather disorganized life. And they were, like Harry Sacher, a great spiritual find.

Here were people with whom problems could be discussed, with whom I could check and verify my ideas, and gauge how they would impress others. Not knowing the great difficulties in our way, they were readier than I, who was often hesitant and overcautious. In short, they helped to make Manchester, the city to which I had come as a stranger, and had considered a place of exile, a happy place for me.'

He goes on later, when discussing the growing burden of the job, to point out Simon's ever-increasing involvement in the cause:

'The office of the English Federation was useless for our purpose. It was out in Fulbourne Street, in the East End. After much consideration and heart-searching we decided to open an office at 175 Piccadilly, and Simon Marks, who was released from military service for this purpose, took charge of it. From that time on our work assumed more organized and systematic form. The little office in Piccadilly became an important centre towards which gravitated everything in Zionist life.'

In November 1952 Chaim Weizmann died while still in office and Simon attended his funeral at Rehovot. Two weeks later a memorial service was held under the auspices of the Zionist Federation at the Albert Hall, at which Simon presided. Israel Finestein, President of the Board of Deputies of British Jews, recalls the occasion precisely: 'Simon got to his feet and had hardly began to speak when he burst into tears.' Such was his sense of loss of the man who must, in many ways, have been a substitute father to him. Simon's friendship with Chaim and Vera Weizmann, like his friendship with Israel Sieff, was of a kind that could only be broken by death. Of Simon, who died twelve years later, Vera wrote: 'He was the greatest friend of my husband and myself for 51 years.' The fortunes of the state of Israel remained close to Simon's heart and his passport shows that he was a frequent visitor there. He continued his financial support of Zionist initiatives.

Simon balanced his giving as far as possible between Jewish and other causes. The £120,000 he donated to the Joint Palestine Appeal prior to his death needs to be seen in the context of the £200,000 he gave to the British Heart Fund. He also gave generously on a personal basis outside the bounds of his Charitable Trust. Senior service officers with whom he had worked during the war and who had now been demobbed, often found themselves in financial straits in the post-war civilian world. A letter from them requesting assistance would immediately be answered with a cheque for £100 or £200. Simon gave little or no consideration to his personal wealth, however, and could be embarrassed by public reference to it. He gave away much more than he spent on his own needs and frequently said, 'I set out to build a business not a fortune'.

Simon's patronage of the Royal College of Surgeons came about through his friendship with the plastic surgeon Archibald Hector McIndoe, who was a frequent guest at Titlarks

ABOVE Simon with Ezer Weizman (Chaim Weizmann's nephew) at a Joint Palestine Association dinner, 1961. Weizman was a hero of the Six-Day War and followed his uncle as President of Israel in 1993.

ABOVE RIGHT Simon and Miriam greeting Geoffrey Fisher, Archbishop of Canterbury, and Israel Brodie, Chief Rabbi.

and at Grosvenor Square. During the war 'Archie' had worked miracles at Queen Victoria Hospital, East Grinstead, where he had repaired the faces and bodies of young air crew who had been burnt – often beyond recognition – in the flames of blazing aircraft. Before the war this handsome, charismatic, New Zealand surgeon had made his living by remodelling the facial features and bodies of rich women; with the advent of war he found a much more important vocation, not only using his skill as a plastic surgeon but helping his young patients psychologically to readjust to normal civilian life. McIndoe's pioneering work in the field of plastic surgery was later to bring him a knighthood.

Simon had met the surgeon through his youngest sister Elaine, whose home was not far from Queen Victoria Hospital. On meeting Archie, Elaine was immediately charmed by him; she joined the hospital's welfare committee and helped to raise large sums to improve the patients' facilities. What is more, she set aside over half her house as a convalescent wing of the hospital. Some of her friends, when visiting her, could not bear the sight of the ravaged young faces and bodies recuperating and simply left, never to return. Elaine introduced McIndoe to Simon, and their subsequent friendship was cemented as it were, by a 'painless' (as Simon demanded) hernia operation performed by McIndoe on Simon in 1944. Archie McIndoe soon became a member of the family's inner circle as well as a confidant; in return, the family – and Simon in particular – strongly supported his medical fund-raising projects.

First came the Marks Fellowships in plastic surgery, then Archie's pet project, the complete rehabilitation of the Royal College of Surgeons building and its training facilities in London (McIndoe was then its Vice-President). Simon would eventually donate over £500,000 to the college, for which in 1957 he was elected an Honorary Fellow and a Member of the Court of Patrons. McIndoe said this of Simon:

'He is among the leaders who have brought the technicians from the back room to the front room. He has always fought against bureaucracy and remote control. He

ABOVE Simon Marks and Archibald Hector McIndoe, the pioneering plastic surgeon who treated the injuries of young air crew badly burnt in blazing aircraft during the Second World War.

ABOVE Invitation to luncheon at Downing Street to meet David Ben Gurion, First Prime Minister of Israel.
ABOVE RIGHT David Ben Gurion in 1952.

has always laid great stress on the importance of good human relationships. Thus he has built up a great firm not as a simple distributing agency for other people's goods but as a highly scientific organization which is a model for all such industries in the world today. Cutting sharply across the bounds of inter-trade jealousies and competitive practices his firm now advises upon the selection and quality of the raw materials used by the manufacturers who supply him. He has improved upon their methods of manufacture and has set standards of quality which have made his business the envy of the world. To do this he has set up a consulting advisory panel of experts whose services are given freely to those who require them. In this, his own field, he has produced a social revolution entirely due to his scientific outlook.'

Simon supported a multitude of charities and good causes. Most importantly he cajoled and coerced other wealthy men to donate generously to deserving causes – preferably to those of his choosing. A favourite saying of his was 'Rich men must learn to give; for some it is the hardest lesson of all and some of them never learn.' When he and Archie McIndoe spotted a wealthy man on the beach at Cannes they would approach him for a donation to some worthy cause. After a time, the approach of Simon and Archie would ensure their quarry's rapid disappearance into the safety of his hotel suite.

In the four years prior to his death in 1964, Simon's known donations via the Simon Marks Charitable Trust totalled over £640,000. He gave £50,000 towards the £100,000 needed to set up a junior department at the King David School, Manchester. In addition

ABOVE Simon and Miriam with friends in Cannes. On Simon's right is the actress Lilli Palmer.

RIGHT Simon and Israel enjoying a Marks & Spencer Head Office party: Lois Sieff, Teddy's wife, is on Israel's right.

he donated several hundred thousand pounds of which no record now exists. Possibly his last recorded gift is one of £7,000 to the Jewish Blind Society. This was presented in the autumn of 1964 by Alec Lerner at the Jewish Blind Society Ball and represented the biggest single contribution to the £17,000 raised.

Neither did he neglect his needy relations. He appointed an executive in the Marks & Spencer building group (who was also a distant relative) to investigate for him whether those on the periphery of the Marks family were financially secure. In addition, Simon helped to ensure that his ageing American cousins, mainly the descendants of his father's brothers and sister, enjoyed a reasonable standard of living by granting them Marks & Spencer shares at discretionary rates.

The arts, too, benefited from Simon's philanthropy. One of his inspirations was the Royal Opera House Benevolent Fund, whose first chairman was Lady Diana Cooper, with Miriam Marks and later Lois Sieff, Teddy's wife, as co-vice-chairmen. Simon personally gave over £50,000 to the fund as well as paying for the grand tier's house lighting. Simon's love of the arts reflected his interest in beautiful objects . . . and people. He liked people who were talented; he liked people who had special gifts and qualities, and above all, he enjoyed the company of attractive men and women. Among his friends were such celebrities as Greer Garson, Lilli Palmer, Joan Fontaine, Rex Harrison and Eddie Fisher. He greatly enjoyed the performing arts, and often compared their disciplines with his work at Marks & Spencer. Once, at the end of a recital by the violinist Isaac Stern, he left the concert hall with tears streaming down his cheeks: 'It made me realize', he said, 'how far we are from perfection in Marks & Spencer.' Similarly, after a performance of *La Bohème* at London's Covent Garden, the sight of the four young people starving in a garret caused him to weep and recall to his guests how the discovery of a hungry sales

Simon at a dinner with his daughter Hannah, sitting opposite.

assistant in one of his stores had prompted the setting up of the company's staff welfare programme.

Simon, now in his late sixties, had one last major contribution to make to the company. One Saturday night, while passing one of his stores on his way home from the office, he saw a light burning at the back of the sales floor. He went into the store, and found two sales assistants busy working. He asked them what they were doing and the girls said, 'Well, Sir, we are counting the stock, as we have to every fortnight.' Simon looked at the cards they were using, saw they were very complicated, and asked the girls, 'Do you really understand all this?' The girls replied, 'No, not really, Sir.' 'Well,' said Simon, 'if you don't understand them, and I am the Chairman of the business, and I don't understand them, there is something wrong with the system.' Within a couple of days a purge was launched under the motto 'If in doubt – cut it out.'

Every form, and every other item of paper, was examined, and if it was not necessary, it was immediately thrown out. After a few months the savings amounted to over 500

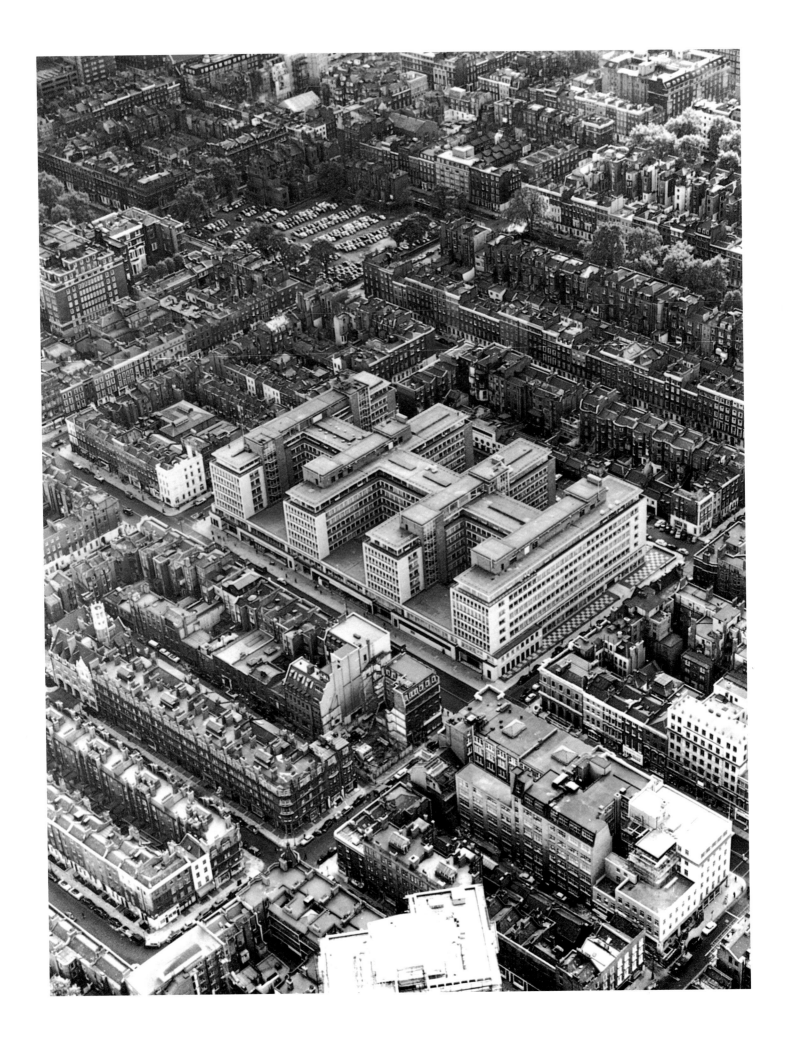

million clerical entries per year. The basis of the new system was 'sensible approximation'; information kept on the off chance that it might be required years later was simply destroyed. The invoicing system with suppliers was revised. Previously, a supplier would issue an invoice to every store that had been sent an item. Each store then checked that it had been received, endorsed the invoice and sent it to Head Office for payment. In other words, the supplier had to raise up to 240 invoices, 240 store staff had to endorse them and send them to Head Office, where some unfortunate person had to collect all 240 together, and then pay them. Following the simplification exercise, the supplier merely sent one invoice to Head Office to cover deliveries of a line to all stores. A check was made with twenty or thirty stores, and then this one invoice was paid.

ABOVE The post room in Head Office where large quantities of incoming and outgoing mail were handled daily.

This streamlining approach was applied right through the organization and as a result the company was able to scrap eighteen million forms, saving eighty tons of paper, a year. The exercise saved enormous amounts of staff time, which in turn meant saving money and, as Simon explained, 'In this business every penny saved is a pound', because there were the same number of pence to the pound as there were stores in the chain. The savings in overheads were passed on in lower prices to the customers, who over two years benefited to the tune of £4 million. There was another benefit, too. Wherever possible the new approach substituted personal contact for remote control, and staff were treated with greater trust and respect. 'Clocking in' was abolished, and the company sold its 240 time clocks.

However, the operation was not achieved without some pain. A number of people were made redundant; some young people who had been promised jobs found the promise withdrawn, and in what became his increasingly irascible style in his latter days, Simon accused one senior director of 'stealing from him' as a result of allowing administration and the costs thereof to escalate.

In 1957 the company mounted a 'Simplification Exhibition', which received considerable publicity, not only in the national but also in the international press. Representatives of 5,000 commercial and industrial organizations in the UK, the Commonwealth, the USA and the Continent visited it. In addition, there were representatives from numerous government departments and local authorities as well as from hospital boards and research institutions. Hugh Fraser MP quoted 'Operation Simplification' in the House as an example for all government departments.

In 1958 the streamlining of Marks & Spencer was taken a stage further by bringing the various head office operations together under one roof in new and spacious premises in Baker Street – which they still occupy today. Thus the physical components were in place for a highly centralized organization, every part of which bore the individual stamp of Simon Marks. The actual fitting out and furnishing of the new offices revealed Simon at his most demanding. In his quest for the perfect office environment, he kept changing his mind about which furniture he wanted or which pictures. So much so that Norman Symes, the executive in charge of the move, eventually had to take sick leave because of nervous exhaustion. Symes also suffered physical exhaustion at the chairman's hand. A few days after the move, Simon Marks used one of the new toilets and found it would not flush. The call went out for Symes, who was given a terrible dressing-down and told to test every toilet in the building. This he did, coming back two hours later with his arm

LEFT The building (centre) that was to become the new Michael House, Baker Street Head Office of Marks & Spencer from 1958 to the present day.

almost needing splints and telling the world that the cistern that the Chairman had used was the only faulty one.

In 1959 Simon was proud to hold his Annual General Meeting in the new offices. In spite of the size and prestige of the company, it was still possible to hold it on the premises. Today, the AGM takes place in a major London hotel and commands an audience approaching 1,500 people. Simon's first duty at that meeting in 1959 was to mark the breaking of the family link with the Spencer family with the announcement of the death, in her ninety-ninth year, of Agnes Spencer, who two years earlier had very generously donated £400,000 to the Marks and Spencer Benevolent Trust. A room was named after her in Hannah House (named after Simon's mother), opened three years previously, a short walk from Michael House. This new building existed purely for the needs of the staff – dining room, rest rooms, changing rooms, showers, etc. – and was open in the evenings for refreshment and recreation. It was characteristic of Simon that the idea for Hannah House came to him when he was thousands of miles away. 'I was deeply impressed when I was in America,' he said, 'by seeing Tennessee Williams's *The Glass Menagerie* and realizing what a terrible effect loneliness can have on people. When I came back I determined to help people overcome it.'

Simon Marks achieved considerable recognition in his lifetime. In 1961 he received a hereditary peerage and took the title 'Lord Marks of Broughton', Broughton being the district of Manchester from which the family – to whose roots it was intended to pay tribute – hailed. 'I was delighted to be given a knighthood,' he observed, 'I fancied myself as a knight succouring distressed maidens. A peerage rather reminds me of old, bad

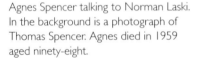

Agnes Spencer talking to Norman Laski. In the background is a photograph of Thomas Spencer. Agnes died in 1959 aged ninety-eight.

ABOVE Lord Marks of Broughton in his robes on the occasion of his introduction to the House of Lords in 1961.

barons.' In his maiden speech in the Lords, he spoke of how improvements in productivity could make lower prices possible, which in turn would make the country more competitive. The following year he received the Tobé Award, the first time this major USA retailing award had ever been bestowed on anyone outside that country. The citation read:

> 'It is no longer possible to distinguish between the upper, middle and lower classes of English society in their dress. Over the years, a team of scientists, technologists and production engineers have been employed to investigate the use of materials, colours and finishes. Manufacturing processes are studied by food technologists who achieve high quality foodstuffs. By such methods Lord Marks has kept his firm in the forefront. He has followed a policy of creating happy working conditions and by treating his employees as responsible members of the Organisation.'

Israel Sieff was to be elevated to the peerage five years later, but as a life baron. His son Marcus became a peer in his own right.

During 1964 Simon spent some time in hospital with heart problems, but this did not prevent him from presiding at his final AGM in March 1964 when once again he was able to report improved figures. Sales that year were over £200 million, and profit before tax over £25 million. Since he had taken over the chairmanship in 1916, sales had grown some five-hundredfold, profits nearly a thousandfold. Despite this continued success, however, Simon's failing health was making him increasingly testy. He could be unmerciful in the office to members of his staff whom he saw failing to measure up to the high standards he consistently set the business. He once sent for John Fry, Executive of the Men's Group, with a query about some men's pyjamas. Not satisfied with a verbal

RIGHT Lord Marks at Manchester University Founder's Day, 1962.

explanation, Simon insisted on seeing them on and told Fry to model them. Fry accordingly stepped out of his clothing and put the pyjamas on in Simon's office. The discussion over, Simon dismissed Fry, who turned to change back into his suit. Simon looked up from his desk, 'What are you doing?' he asked. 'I am changing back into my clothes, Sir,' said Fry. 'This is not a bloody changing room, get out!', Simon snapped, and Fry had to go out into the corridor with the pyjamas on and his suit over his arm. Stories like this were told with rueful pride by the people concerned and paraded with honour like war wounds.

On 8 December 1964, the day before the general staff Christmas lunch, Simon (then aged seventy-six) went to inspect items in the Ladies Tailoring Department. He was less than pleased with the quality of some of the merchandise he was shown, and in making his usual complaint that they were ruining his business, hurled garments to the floor and to the distress of the members of the department stormed out accompanied by his favourite nephew and group director, Michael Sieff. The pair then went to a large office on the first floor to inspect proposed post-Christmas reductions assembled there for Simon's scrutiny. As they entered the room, Michael Sieff felt a hand on his shoulder as Simon slumped against him and fell to the floor. He had suffered a massive and fatal heart attack. Michael rushed to summon help. Dr Alec Lerner, Simon's son-in-law and putative heir, was called. Although he applied mouth-to-mouth resuscitation, he knew immediately that there was no hope. To Michael's distressed pleas to fetch the oxygen cylinder from Simon's office or to apply heart massage, Alec said quietly, 'Michael, there is nothing to be done. He is an old man, let him rest in peace.'

Simon's death occurred soon after lunch. During the course of the afternoon, the news spread through the building – and the business. The members of the Ladies Tailoring Department were distraught. It was, of course, no fault of theirs (although their executive was later to be told by a director that he was responsible for Simon's death). Simon had been suffering from heart disease for some time and had continued to work – unwisely, perhaps – at his usual relentless pace.

The next day, the board assembled the executives of the business to address them. An emotional Israel Sieff made what was almost an apologia for Simon, acknowledging that he had been very difficult in his later years, but emphasizing that he always meant well and acted out of love for the business. As the emotion of the loss of his lifelong partner got the better of him, his voice tailed off and the Company Secretary, Bruce Goodman, brought the meeting to an end by standing up and quoting from the Bible, 'to your tents, Oh Israel'. Marcus Sieff said later, 'I have no doubt that if he could have exercised a choice it would have been to end as he did, without pain at work in his business.'

Simon Marks had been Chairman of Marks & Spencer through four reigns and almost half a century. In that time he turned a successful chain of bazaars into a national institution. He had been the rightful heir to the business that his father had created but he had to struggle to gain control of it – and once he had that control he carried his birthright like a sacred trust, striving to perfect the business with a zeal and a certainty of purpose that were almost religious. This he did without faltering until, literally, the day he died.

The funeral took place two days later at the Golders Green Crematorium in northwest London. The fact that he was cremated caused some raised eyebrows in the Jewish community; notwithstanding Simon's lack of religious commitment, cremation was then and remains still, unacceptable in the Orthodox Jewish establishment. Indeed, among the

Simon Marks, the unassuming head of a retail empire, standing in front of a display of St Michael men's shirts and underwear.

many tributes in the *Jewish Chronicle*, there is no mention of the funeral itself. Reference, however, to the records of Kenyons, the undertakers, reveals a simple handwritten entry:

MARKS, Rt. Hon. Lord	Cremate
Motor Hearse	G. G.
4 men	10/30
Crem. Fees	Own Rabbi
Meds.	Ashes T/D

This simple epitaph tells of a 10.30 a.m. cremation at Golders Green, with Kenyons supplying the hearse and four operatives, but not the rabbi (the funeral service was conducted by the Reverend Ephraim Levine, an old family friend). 'Meds' refers to medical fees involved – preparation of the body – and 'Ashes T/D' indicates 'temporary disposal'. Simon's ashes, in fact, remain to this day at rest in Golders Green.

Two subsequent memorial meetings were held. One was a religious service at the New West End Synagogue, Bayswater, conducted by Ephraim Levine. This was followed by a memorial meeting at the Friends Meeting House in Euston in London, organized by the Zionist Organisation of Great Britain. It was attended by over 600 people, with speakers including Julian Amery MP, Barnett Janner and Manny Shinwell MP. Shinwell, a doughty socialist Glaswegian Jew who had had no significant contact with the Jewish community in particular, felt moved nonetheless to say that Simon Marks had 'helped suppress the foul cancer of anti-Semitism'.

There were also innumerable press tributes to Simon throughout December. *The Times* obituary was headed 'Lord Marks of Broughton – The Retail Revolution'. *The Financial Times* called him 'The Genius of the Retail Trade'. A leading article in the *Sun* said: 'He was an inspiration – one who believed in giving value for money, and who blasted through every sort of obstruction to do it.' The *Daily Express* wrote: 'He brought high fashion within the reach of every typist and shop assistant and filled the streets of Britain with prettily dressed women . . . His concern for his staff was not only fatherly. It was also generous.'

An obituary notice in the *Jewish Chronicle* records that Simon had represented the Birkenhead Synagogue at the Board of Deputies of British Jews. The board's records show that Simon was a member from 1917 to 1935. It is still not uncommon for people living in London to represent a provincial community, thus saving the time and expense of sending a representative. It is reasonable to assume, however, that Simon's main motive in coming to the board was to support (pre-Balfour Declaration) the strong Zionist school of thought opposing the non-Zionist and anti-Zionist attitudes of the leaders of the board at the time. His sister, Becky, Israel Sieff's wife, became a member of the Board of Deputies in the year immediately following World War II. She is recalled by Judge Israel Finestein, the current President of the board: 'They were', he says, 'no more than four or five women on the Board and I remember Becky Sieff very clearly. She must have represented WIZO [Women's International Zionist Organisation] but it was clear to everybody that she actually represented the family.' Judge Finestein also comments on the uniqueness of this basically non-religious trading family holding such a major place in the Jewish community and spearheading moves to counter the anti-Zionism of many of the old Anglo-Jewish establishment.

Simon died a multi-millionaire but his widow, Miriam, fearing that the money would run out, kept over a million pounds on current account deposit in a small local branch of Barclays Bank. The manager – understandably – was worried about this amount of cash

St Michael NEWS

LORD MARKS OF BROUGHTON 1888-1964

MARKS of BROUGHTON.—On December 8th, 1964, suddenly in London, SIMON—LORD MARKS OF BROUGHTON, beloved husband of Miriam and father of Michael and Hannah. Funeral private.

The announcement was appropriately simple.

Lord Marks of Broughton will be remembered as the kindly genius who touched all our lives. With a kind of magic. Now the genius is gone. But the magic lives on. And in this commemorative issue we salute the man who worked it. Below is an appreciation of Lord Marks by Israel Sieff, his brother-in-law, his life-long colleague, his successor as Chairman of Marks & Spencer.

The kindly genius

Simon Marks was my brother-in-law and my mentor for nearly fifty years. More than that, since the time when as young boys we went daily to Manchester Grammar School together, he was my beloved friend.

In this issue of *St. Michael News*, which is devoted to his memory, you will read many wonderful tributes paid to him in the Press and by his friends. I would like to draw attention to two of his especially remarkable qualities which impressed those of us who were closest to him. The first was the gift of simplicity. He had no use for complexities of language and ideas. Simple in his approach, he cut right across involved verbiage and went to the heart of those problems which were exercising his mind. His second characteristic was a deep sensitivity. He had a rare flair—an ability to sense a situation. He possessed an intuitive brilliance which helped to make him unique in the business world.

To all our employees he was like a father with his children, and though a perfectionist himself, he was very protective towards people who were less so.

We shall carry on the business in the spirit he inculcated into us with so much inspiration and affection. This business will continue to grow and develop, founded as it is on a philosophy formulated by our guide and our teacher, the late Simon Marks. May God rest his soul in peace.

that he held for Lady Marks and at least once a week would ring her and ask if she would like to withdraw some money. He often collected her from Titlarks and drove her to the bank in the hope that she would. Lady Marks died in 1971 at the age of seventy-seven.

In his final years, Simon had become more and more anxious that the principles on which he had developed the business would be eroded. This led to him taking the company under an ever tighter and more restrictive rein. Israel Sieff, his natural successor and right-hand man for thirty-eight years, loosened the reins a little and allowed some developments that Lord Marks had suppressed. In his memoirs, written five years after Simon's death, Israel (then Lord Sieff) reflected as objectively as a friend can on the nature of his partner's contribution to retailing:

> '... what I admired in him most was the clarity of his purposes and the directness with which he went out to achieve them. He found himself running a chain of penny bazaars and wanted to convert it into a chain of superstores. He did it. He was egotistic enough to want his goods to have a distinct quality, second to none, and accepted as such by the nation. He got this. The brand name "St Michael" means something to everybody who shops in Marks and Spencer: if they knew it, they would know it means above all Simon. Above all he wanted to forward his enterprise on a philanthropic attitude to human relations, on the notion of trust and service and progress. He did that too.
>
> ... The ultimate key to the success of Marks and Spencer was peculiarly Simon's contribution: his instinctive judgement for what the people wanted. Our feats of adaptation to change of demand could never have been so swiftly executed had Simon's sense of how things were changing not been so highly developed and reliable. He rode the market like a jockey rides a great race – sensing what is happening before anybody else does, and boldly and swiftly acting on his judgement.'

Simon's two great interests – aside from his beloved Marks & Spencer – were the human condition and Zionism. He made a unique contribution to both. His approach to good human relations both within the business and beyond ensured an improvement in living standards for innumerable people, from individuals within his own family to tens of thousands of families of his own employees. His philanthropy and powers of fund-raising set new levels for these activities. His passion for Zionism, and his support, with Israel Sieff, for Chaim Weizmann, unquestioningly played an indispensable and seminal part in the foundation of the state of Israel. He was at the head of a tradition of British support for Israel and her institutions which continues in these materialistic times.

The greatest legacy that Simon Marks left is the spirit with which he imbued Marks & Spencer and which lives on in the business today. As Sir Richard Greenbury, the present Chairman, puts it:

> 'He established principles which are today as important to our success as when he was establishing them, so he didn't just leave a great business he left the means by which it could continue to be a great business ... He was a remarkable man in that he didn't just have great vision and know where he was going, he had the capacity to run every part of this business and know how to get what he wanted out of the business ... but for me the great single thing I have to say about him is that what he built just carried on and carries on long after his death and we all still believe in what he believed in.'

Many of the innovations that he brought to the high street were revolutionary but then, as Simon Marks himself liked to repeat, 'I am the greatest rebel of you all.'

Tribute to Lord Marks in *St Michael News*, the Marks & Spencer staff newspaper, following his death on 8 December 1964.

Index

PHOTOGRAPHIC ACKNOWLEDGEMENTS

Marks & Spencer and the publishers would like to thank the following sources for their help in providing illustrations for the book: Imperial War Museum, pp. 128, 130; Jewish Chronicle Library, p. 51; Public Record Office p. 33.

The Archivist is grateful to members of the family and staff of the company who have very kindly donated photographs to the collection, many of which have been reproduced in this book.